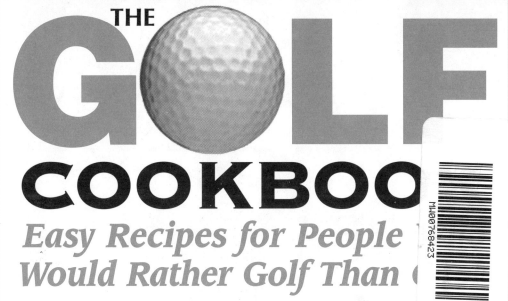

THE GOLF
COOKBOOK

Easy Recipes for People
Would Rather Golf Than C

Sharon Gerardi & Nadine Neme

REDBANK RANCH CLOVIS, CALIFORNI

THE GOLF COOKBOOK

Easy Recipes for People Who Would Rather Golf Than Cook
by Sharon Gerardi and Nadine Nemechek

Published by:
Redbank Ranch
10683 E. Bullard Ave
Clovis, CA 93611 U.S.A.

Manufactured in the United States of America
Library of Congress Cataloguing-in Publication Data
Gerardi, Sharon and Nemechek, Nadine
The Golf Cookbook
Easy Recipes for People Who Would Rather Golf Than Cook

p.cm.

1. Cookery, American 2. Golf, Tips, Trivia—Recipes I. Title
Library of Congress Catalog Card Number 98-91266

1st Printing 1998
2nd Printing 2000

ISBN 0-9657500-1-9

Printed in the USA by
WIMMER
The Wimmer Companies
Memphis

FROM THE TEE TO THE TABLE

The STARTER (cocktails and appetizers) 5

HOLE #1 CHIP SHOT (chips and dips) 17

HOLE #2 WATER HAZARDS (soups and chili) 25

HOLE #3 The GREENS (salads) 33

HOLE #4 BIRDIES and EAGLES (chicken and turkey) 45

HOLE #5 The HOOK and the SANDTRAP (fish and shellfish) 61

HOLE #6 The SHANK and the LINKS (meat and sausage) 73

HOLE #7 The MULLIGAN (stews, casseroles, and pasta) 93

HOLE #8 The CLUB and the SLICE (sandwiches, pizza, and bread) 111

HOLE #9 The SWEET SPOT (desserts) 127

4

We dedicate this book to all golfers. May all your drives be long
and all your putts be true and may you never find yourself in the rough.

Special thanks to
Vic Nemechek, and Joe, Michael, John, and Christine Gerardi.

The Starter
(cocktails and appetizers)

GOLFER'S MARTINI

A   1 wood of gin (1½ ounces)
A   5 iron of lemon vodka (½ ounce)

A   sand wedge of dry vermouth (a splash)

Stir with cracked ice; strain into cocktail glass; add olive or lemon peel.

GOLF QUOTATION: "Income tax has made liars out of more Americans than golf."

Will Rogers

19TH HOLE MANHATTAN COCKTAIL

From a bartender at the old Olympic Club in San Francisco.

1½ ounces (1 jigger) good bourbon
1½ ounces (1 jigger) sweet vermouth
1 dash Angostura Bitters

1 drop grenadine syrup
1 stemmed maraschino cherry

Place 4 medium ice cubes in a mixing glass. Add all ingredients, wait for 10 seconds, and stir with a long mixing spoon for 5 seconds. Strain into an ice cold stemmed cocktail glass and add an stemmed cherry impaled on a toothpick. Yield: 1 cocktail

GOLF RULES: A ball played from the green that hits the flagstick carries a 2 shot penalty.

GOLFER'S PUNCH

Perfect after 18 on a warm day.

1 cup iced tea
1 cup orange juice
2 cups pineapple juice

2 cups chilled ginger ale
2 pints pineapple or orange sherbet

Before you leave for the course combine the tea, orange juice, and pineapple juice and refrigerate. When the thirsty golfers return, place in a punch bowl, add the ginger ale, and float scoops of sherbet on top. Yield: 14 servings

GOLF QUOTATION: "Give me golf clubs, fresh air, and a beautiful partner, and you can keep the golf clubs and the fresh air."

Jack Benny

PRIZE MONEY PUNCH

½ cup orange liqueur or brandy
2 oranges, thinly sliced
2 lemons, thinly sliced
¼ cup sugar

1 bottle dry red or white wine
½ cup orange juice
2 cups club soda
  Orange and lemon slices

In a large pitcher combine the orange liqueur, oranges, lemons, and sugar, pressing on the fruit. Let mixture stand for 30 minutes. Add wine and orange juice and let stand another 30 minutes. To serve stir well and add club soda. Serve in tall glasses with ice and slices of orange and lemon. Yield: 4 servings

GOLF EQUIPMENT: There are two single-use golf-specific 35 mm pocket cameras. One comes plain and the other (Kodak's Fairway Performance) comes with captions such as "Wild about golf!"

WAIKIKI 19TH HOLE MAI TAI

Created by Trader Vic, this concoction tasted so great, his Tahitian friends exclaimed, "Mai Tai" which means "out of this world!" Every bartender in the tropics has his own secret recipe.

3   ounces pineapple juice
3   ounces orange juice
3   ounces lemon juice
1½ ounces light rum

½   ounce curaçao
1½ ounces dark rum
    Maraschino cherries or a
    spear of fresh pineapple

Combine the first 5 ingredients, pour over crushed ice, and stir. Float the dark rum on top and garnish with the cherries or pineapple. Yield: 2 drinks

GOLF TRAVEL: Only 5 minutes from Waikiki, Ala Wai Golf Course is the most played links-style course in the nation.

"LOST BALL" SAUSAGE AND CHEESE APPETIZER

These can be made ahead, "lost" in the freezer, and baked when needed.

2¼ cups baking mix
12 ounces pork sausage
3 cups shredded cheddar cheese

¾ teaspoon dry mustard
⅛ teaspoon cayenne

Preheat oven to 350 degrees. Mix all the ingredients well (you can use a mixer or food processor for this). Shape into 1-inch balls. Place on a baking sheet that has been sprayed with no-stick cooking spray. Bake 25 minutes. Serve warm. Yield: about 54 appetizers

GOLF GREATS: In 1960 Arnold Palmer charged to victory with a final round of 65 in the U.S. Open at Cherry Hills in Colorado. He won 6 times in 1960 and changed the game forever.

SUDDEN DEATH SAUSAGES

This will get everyone's attention.

½ cup sauerkraut
1 cup chili sauce
1 cup beer
2 teaspoons brown sugar

2 teaspoons caraway seeds
2 packages (16 ounces each) cocktail
  sausages

Remove the sauerkraut from the can to the measuring cup with a fork. Do not rinse or drain. Put in a blender or food processor with the rest of the ingredients except the sausages. Blend until smooth. Transfer to a small saucepan and simmer. Add sausages and keep warm for serving in a chafing dish or slow cooker. Serve with cocktail forks or toothpicks. Yield: 20 servings

GOLF TOURNAMENTS: The AT&T Pebble Beach National Pro-Am is the only PGA Tour-sponsored pro-am in which amateurs can continue playing until the last putt drops on Sunday.

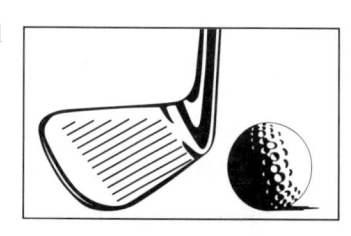

BEST BALL BROILED AVOCADO APPETIZER

1 ripe avocado   Your favorite barbecue sauce
   Butter, melted   Crackers

Preheat the broiler. Cut the avocado in half and remove the seed. Brush with the melted butter and the barbecue sauce. Broil 3 to 5 minutes until slightly brown. Spread on crackers for serving. Yield: 4 servings

GOLF QUOTATION: "The golf course is the last place to learn how to play golf."

Unknown

SHORT GAME SQUARES

These are a good cold snack too. Cut larger squares, wrap in foil, and take some along in your golf bag.

2 cups cooked rice
1 can (4 ounces) diced green chiles
3 cups shredded Jack cheese
4 tablespoons chopped pimento or roasted red peppers

2 tablespoons chopped olives
6 eggs, slightly beaten
1 teaspoon salt

Preheat oven to 350 degrees. Combine all the ingredients in a bowl. Pour into a 13 x 9-inch baking dish that has been sprayed with no-stick cooking spray. Bake for 30 minutes or until set. Cut into 1¼-inch squares. Serve warm or cold. Can be made ahead and warmed in the microwave. Yield: 70 squares

GOLF DECISION: Paper or plastic? Spikes or spikeless? By mid-1997 the number of golf courses that banned metal spikes had jumped to 150 including 10 that hold LPGA tour events.

STARTING TIME CRAB FU YUNG

It's your turn to serve cocktails and hors d'oeuvres. Try something different!

¾ cup finely chopped bell pepper
½ cup finely chopped onion
2 teaspoons oil
1 can (6 ounces) crab meat, drained
1 cup fresh or canned bean sprouts, drained

5 eggs, beaten
1 tablespoon cornstarch
1 tablespoon soy sauce
½ teaspoon salt
¼ teaspoon cayenne

Cook the bell pepper and onion in the oil until soft, transfer to a bowl, and add the rest of the ingredients. Mix well. Drop by tablespoonfuls onto a hot griddle that has been sprayed with no-stick cooking spray and brown on both sides. Keep warm in a low oven. Serve on small plates with Chinese plum sauce and hot Chinese mustard. Yield: 8 servings

GOLF WINNERS: In 1997 on the LPGA Tour the 4 major winners had an average age of 39, while younger stars (average age 27) were the major winners on the PGA Tour.

PIN POSITION PITA BREAD GOAT CHEESE PIZZETTES

A delicious and easy appetizer.

6   (6-inch) pita bread rounds
3   thinly sliced ripe tomatoes
2   bell peppers, sliced into thin rounds

Salt and pepper
4   ounces goat cheese
Grated Parmesan cheese

Place the pita breads on a cookie sheet. Top each with the tomatoes. Don't overlap. Add some bell pepper rings. Lightly salt and pepper the vegetables. Crumble some goat cheese over each one and sprinkle with the Parmesan cheese. Broil 8 inches from the heat until brown and bubbly. Cut each pita bread into 4 pieces. Yield: 24 appetizers

GOLF GREATS: Kelly Robbins recorded the lowest 4-round score in LPGA history as she won the 1997 Jamie Farr Classic in Sylvana, Georgia with a score of 265.

HOLE #1

Chip Shot (chips and dips)

2 PUTT PITA CHIPS

Tasty chips for dips or plain with cocktails.

½ cup (1 stick) soft butter
2 tablespoons chopped fresh parsley or
    1 teaspoon dried
1 tablespoon finely chopped chives or
    green onions

1 tablespoon lemon juice
¼ teaspoon garlic powder
1 teaspoon lemon pepper seasoning
6 pita breads, split in half horizontally

Preheat oven to 400 degrees. Blend all the ingredients except pita into a paste. Spread each pita bread half with the butter paste and cut into wedge-shaped quarters. Place on 2 cookie sheets not overlapping and bake for 5 to 7 minutes until crispy and slightly brown. Yield: 48 chips

GOLF QUOTATION: "The only time my prayers are never answered is on the golf course."

Billy Graham

CHEATER'S 5 MINUTE SALSA

Your company will think you chopped for hours.

1 can (28 ounces) whole peeled tomatoes
1 bunch cilantro, well washed, stems removed
3 green onions, cut in 1-inch pieces
3 garlic cloves
3 whole pickled jalapeños (or 1 for wimps)
1 tablespoon juice from jalapeño jar
1 teaspoon ground cumin
1 teaspoon salt

Put all the ingredients in a food processor or blender and pulse until desired consistency. Serve with tortilla chips. Yield: about 3½ cups

GOLF HEALTH: Walking the course can have real health benefits. Be sure to use a modern designed lightweight golf bag. These newer bags are less likely to cause back pain.

TRIPLE DIP FOR CHIPS

2   cups salsa   2   cups sour cream
2   cups frozen guacamole, thawed

Layer equal amounts of salsa, guacamole, and sour cream in a pretty clear glass bowl.
Yield: 8 to 10 servings

G⃝LF HEALTH: Golfers experiencing pains from overexertion, strain, or even arthritis are
turning to magnet therapy in large numbers. According to *Golf Illustrated Magazine*, magnet
therapy has been proven to relieve pain, improve circulation, and accelerate healing.

GOOD GRIP GUACAMOLE

Double or triple this recipe. You can never have too much.

1   ripe avocado
¼   cup finely chopped white onion
1   jalapeño, seeded and finely chopped

1   tablespoon chopped cilantro
1   small tomato, chopped
    Salt

Mash the avocado, but not too smooth (leave a little chunky). Add the rest of the ingredients and refrigerate for 1 hour for flavors to blend. Serve with tortilla chips and Mexican beer. Yield: 4 servings

GOLF ODDITY: The greatest left-handed golfer, Bob Charles, is naturally right-handed. He began playing left-handed because his parents did and had some spare clubs.

CHIPPY CHILI DIP

Better double the recipe. Golfers have been known to eat this with a spoon.

1   can (15 ounces) chili without beans   ½   cup salsa
½   tablespoon chili powder   1   can (4 ounces) sliced black olives

Mix all the ingredients and heat in the microwave or on the top of the stove. Serve warm with large corn chips. Put out little plates and spoons. Yield: about 3 cups

GOLF STATISTICS: 42% of women golfers play golf to spend more time with their families.

THE COURSE CURRY DIP

A delicious dip for vegetable crudités.

1   package (8 ounces) whipped cream
     cheese
½ cup sour cream
3 tablespoons lemon juice

1   teaspoon garlic salt
½ cup chopped onion
1½ teaspoons curry powder
⅛ teaspoon cayenne, optional

Let the cream cheese soften at room temperature. Blend in the rest of the ingredients.
Yield: about 2 cups

GOLF STATISTICS: 61% of female golfers say they have taken lessons,
while only 42% of male golfers say they've had formal instruction.

CHIP SHOT

DRIVING RANGE DIP

A lady practicing at the driving range gave me this recipe.
She must have been a gourmet.

1   envelope (1.8 ounces) leek soup mix
1   pint sour cream

1   package (3 ounces) smoked salmon, cut
     into small strips
     Chopped fresh parsley or dill

Mix the soup mix, sour cream, and salmon. Refrigerate several hours to blend flavors.
Garnish with parsley or dill. Serve with bagel chips or 2 Putt Pita Chips. Yield: 2 cups

GOLF QUIZ: What is a "chili dip"?

ANSWER: A "chili dip" occurs when the clubhead strikes the ground behind the ball producing a weak short shot.

HOLE #2

Water Hazards (soups and chili)

FREEZER TO FOURSOME HAMBURGER SOUP

*You invited the gang over for your famous hamburger soup
but forgot to thaw the meat. Not to worry.*

1 pint water
1 pound frozen hamburger
1 quart vegetable juice
1 can (28 ounces) diced tomatoes
4 beef bouillon cubes

2 medium onions, thinly sliced
1 bag (24 ounces) frozen stew vegetables
1 package (10 ounces) frozen peas
Salt and pepper

Put all the ingredients in a soup kettle and simmer covered for 1½ hours. Break up the meat into small pieces and simmer 30 minutes longer. Yield: 6 servings

GOLF QUIZ: What is a "dunch"?

ANSWER: A dunch is a low, running shot played with either a wood or iron club.

DOUBLE BOGEY BLACK BEANS AND HOT ITALIAN SAUSAGE

So you had a bad round—this hearty soup will make you forget all about it.

1 onion, chopped
1 bell pepper, chopped
2 teaspoons chopped garlic from a jar
1 tablespoon olive oil
2 cans (15 ounces each) black beans, undrained
1 can (15 ounces) black beans, undrained and puréed in a blender

4 cups chicken broth
8 ounces hot Italian sausage, sliced into 1-inch rounds
1 teaspoon ground cumin
½ teaspoon (or more) red pepper flakes
¼ cup sherry
Salt and pepper

In a large saucepan cook the onion, bell pepper, and garlic in the oil until soft. Add the beans, puréed beans, broth, sausage, cumin, and red pepper flakes to taste. Bring to a boil, reduce heat, and simmer covered for 30 minutes. Add the sherry and salt and pepper if needed. Serve in bowls with crusty bread. Yield: 6 servings

GOLF CHARITIES: The GTE Byron Nelson Classic, won by Tiger Woods in 1997, is among the few events that give more to charity than to the players.

EL NIÑO SAUSAGE SOUP

Causes global warming. Good after a chilly early morning round.
Make it the day before—it will only increase in flavor.

4   cans (11.5 ounces each) spicy or picante vegetable juice
1   can (28 ounces) diced tomatoes
2   packages (10 ounces each) frozen vegetables

2   teaspoons dried basil
1   teaspoon dried oregano
1   teaspoon sugar
1½ pounds Italian sausage, casings removed and crumbled

Put all the ingredients in a large pot, bring to a boil, reduce heat, and simmer for 1½ hours. Yield: 6 servings

GOLF TRAVEL: Sotogrande in Spain's Costa del Sol region is usually cited among the top 10 courses to play in Europe.

BACK NINE BOUILLABAISSE

On the back nine you invited your foursome for dinner.
This gourmet soup can be ready in less than an hour.

½ cup chopped onion
½ cup chopped bell pepper
1 garlic clove, crushed
2 tablespoons butter
2 cups tomato juice
1 cup water
¼ cup lemon juice

½ teaspoon dried thyme
1 can (6 ounces) crab meat, drained
1 package (6 ounces) refrigerated
   imitation lobster
1 can (4¼ ounces) shrimp, drained
   Salt and pepper

Cook the onion, bell pepper, and garlic in the butter in a saucepan over low heat until soft. Add the tomato juice, water, lemon juice, and thyme. Bring to a boil, reduce heat, and simmer covered 15 minutes. Break up the seafood into chunks and add to the tomato mixture. Simmer until hot through. Taste for salt and pepper. Serve with a tossed green salad and crusty bread. Yield: 4 servings

GOLF GREATS: Chi-Chi Rodriguez, always very talkative, was known in his younger days as "the clown prince of the Tour".

"SO YOU WHIFFED IT" BEAN AND HOMINY CHILI

Console yourself with this "hot as a pistol", and easy to make vegetarian chili.

1 can (28 ounces) diced tomatoes
1 can (28 ounces) pinto beans, undrained
1 can (28 ounces) hominy, drained
1 cup water
2 teaspoons ground cumin
2 tablespoons chili powder

1 teaspoon salt
1 jalapeño, chopped (for milder taste remove seeds)
1 bell pepper, chopped
1 onion, chopped
2 teaspoons crushed garlic

Put everything in a large pot. Simmer covered for 30 minutes. If it gets too thick, add a little more water. Serve with warm tortillas and cold Mexican beer. Yield: 4 to 6 servings

GOLF QUIZ: What is golf spelled backwards?

"BURNING UP THE COURSE" CHILI BEANS

½ pound hot links sausages, sliced into
    rounds
1 tablespoon butter
1 large onion, chopped
2 garlic cloves, crushed
1 large bell pepper, chopped
2 cans (15 ounces each) pinto beans,
    undrained

3 cups water
1 teaspoon ground cumin
1 tablespoon chili powder
1 teaspoon dried oregano
1 can (28 ounces) diced tomatoes
1 teaspoon salt
½ teaspoon pepper

In a large pot brown the sausage in the butter. Add the onion, garlic, and bell pepper and cook over low heat until the vegetables are soft. Add the beans, water, cumin, chili powder, oregano, tomatoes, salt, and pepper and simmer covered for 30 minutes. Taste for seasonings. Serve in wide bowls with big spoons. Accompany with chopped onions, grated cheese, and warm flour tortillas. Yield: 4 to 6 servings

GOLF QUOTATION: "Golf is a good walk spoiled."

Mark Twain

AMATEUR TITLE AVOCADO SOUP

A cold soup after a hot round.

1½ cucumbers
3 avocados
3 cups chicken broth
¾ cup light sour cream

3 tablespoons lemon juice
1½ teaspoons salt
Dash Tabasco
3 tomatoes

Peel the cucumbers, cut in half, scrape out the seeds, and cut into chunks. Purée all the ingredients except the tomatoes in a blender or food processor. Chill. Dip the tomatoes in boiling water for 10 seconds to loosen the peel. Peel and dice the tomatoes. Serve the soup in chilled bowls and garnish with the diced tomatoes. Accompany with crusty bread. Yield: 6 servings

GLAMOUR GOLF: Blonde-haired Edith Cummings, winner of the 1923 Amateur, was rumored to be the model for one of F. Scott Fitzgerald's beautiful high society women in his novel *The Great Gatsby*.

HOLE #3

The Greens (salads)

OAKMONT CROUTON SALAD

2 slices French bread, cut into cubes	½ cup olive oil
1 cup chopped tomatoes	⅓ cup red wine vinegar
1 cup sliced celery	2 teaspoons garlic salt
¼ cup chopped green or sweet red onions	½ teaspoon pepper
6 cups romaine lettuce, torn in pieces	

Put the bread in the bottom of the salad bowl. Add the vegetables in the order given. Mix the oil, vinegar, garlic salt, and pepper. Just before serving pour the dressing over the salad and toss. Yield: 6 servings

GOLF RULES: In 1987 at Torrey Pines, Craig Stadler, whose ball was under a tree, was disqualified for using a towel to keep his pants dry while playing a shot from his knees, thereby building a stance and violating Rule 13-3.

Pennsylvania

GREENS KEEPER SALAD DRESSING

Make this delicious dressing on a rainy day.
It makes enough for several salads and keeps in the refrigerator for weeks.

1	cup olive oil		1	teaspoon dried basil
1	tablespoon minced onion		1	teaspoon dried oregano
2	tablespoons grated Parmesan cheese		1	teaspoon sugar
3	teaspoons salt		1	teaspoon pepper
1	teaspoon Worcestershire sauce		½	cup red wine vinegar
1	teaspoon dry mustard		2	tablespoons lemon juice

In a blender or food processor blend the olive oil, onion, and Parmesan cheese until smooth. Add the rest of the ingredients and blend for 30 seconds.

GOLF HERO: In 1997 Meadowwood Country Club in Ft. Pierce, Florida joined in Tigermania by changing it's name to Panther Woods.

ROQUEFORT DRESSING FOR LIGHTNING FAST ROMAINE GREENS

2   envelopes (1.2 ounces each) Caesar
    salad dressing mix
¼   cup vinegar
1   tablespoon lemon juice
¾   cup oil

2   tablespoons sugar
¾   cup sour cream
½   cup buttermilk
4   ounces Roquefort cheese,
    crumbled

In a blender blend everything except the Roquefort until smooth. Pour into a bowl or storage container and stir in the cheese. Refrigerate 2 hours to blend flavors. Thin, if necessary, with a little buttermilk. Yield: about 2½ cups

GOLF TRAVEL: British Airways will help you customize a golf vacation in Scotland, including tee times for championship courses.

THE GREATER GREENSBORO SALAD

1 jar (6 ounces) marinated artichoke
    hearts
1 tablespoon lemon juice

½ teaspoon season salt
8 cups crisp salad greens or baby spinach
2 tablespoons grated Parmesan cheese

Drain the artichoke hearts, reserving the marinade. Cut the hearts into bite-size pieces. Combine the marinade with the lemon juice and season salt. In a large salad bowl toss the marinade mixture with the artichokes and salad greens. Sprinkle with the cheese.

Yield: 8 servings

G◯LF QUIZ: Most sand wedges have some degree of bounce. What is bounce?

North Carolina

ANSWER: The trailing edge of the club is lower than the leading edge.

HACKER'S SALAD

½ head iceberg lettuce, torn into 2-inch
   pieces
2 ripe tomatoes, cut in eighths
2 stalks celery, sliced
¼ cup sliced Spanish olives

½ cup julienne strips Swiss cheese
½ cup julienne strips ham or turkey
   Hacker's Dressing (next page)
2 teaspoons grated Romano cheese

Put the vegetables, olives, Swiss cheese, and meat in a very large salad bowl. Using 2 spoons in each hand, hack as you toss the vegetables with the dressing. Continue hacking and tossing until salad is well mixed. (The hacking releases some of the vegetable juices that mix with the dressing.) Add Romano cheese and toss 1 more time. Yield: 4 servings

PUTTING TIP: Have a putting routine. Read the hole; see the line; and roll the ball into the hole.

HACKER'S DRESSING

⅛ cup white wine vinegar
½ cup extra-virgin olive oil
4 garlic cloves, minced
1 teaspoon Worcestershire sauce

1 teaspoon salt
⅛ teaspoon pepper
1 teaspoon dried oregano
2 teaspoons lemon juice

Put all the ingredients in a blender and blend until smooth.

GOLF STATISTICS: 22% of all golfers regularly shoot better than 90 for 18 holes on a regulation course.

MATCH PLAY WARM PASTA SALAD WITH GREENS

8　ounces rotelle or spaghetti
½　cup Always in the Fridge Salad
　　Dressing (next page)

3　Roma tomatoes, cut into quarters
8　cups mixed salad greens
　　Grated Parmesan cheese

Cook the pasta according to package directions. Drain. Return the pasta to the pot, toss with the salad dressing and tomatoes. Arrange the salad greens on 4 large salad plates and top with the pasta/tomato mixture. Drizzle any dressing left in the pot over the greens. Sprinkle with the Parmesan cheese. Yield: 4 main dish salads

GOLF TRAVEL: In Bay St. Louis, Mississippi, a resort town an hour's drive east of New Orleans, The Bridges Golf Course is named for 21 bridges that span more than 4,000 feet of lakes and wetlands.

ALWAYS IN THE FRIDGE SALAD DRESSING

Keep this dressing on hand at all times. It's good on everything!
It can be your own personal "house dressing". Enjoy!

2¼ cups oil
1 cup wine vinegar
2 tablespoons salt
2 tablespoons sugar
1 tablespoon pepper

1 tablespoon MSG, optional (it boosts the flavor)
1 tablespoon Dijon mustard
2 cloves crushed garlic

Blend all the ingredients in a blender or food processor or shake in a quart jar until well blended. Store in the fridge. Shake well before each use. Yield: 3½ cups

GOLF MOM: In 1997 forty-year-old Nancy Lopez, who has 3 daughters, won for the first time since 1993 and just missed capturing her first U.S. Open crown.

PRINCEVILLE KIWI AND PAPAYA SALAD

2   ripe kiwi, peeled and sliced
2   ripe papayas, halved, seeded, peeled,
      and sliced (reserve the seeds)

4   cups shredded lettuce
      Papaya Seed Salad Dressing
        (recipe follows)

Toss the fruits with the lettuce and enough dressing to barely coat. Serve immediately.
Yield: 4 servings

PAPAYA SEED SALAD DRESSING

1   cup sugar
1   tablespoon salt
1   teaspoon dry mustard
1   teaspoon MSG, optional
1   dash Tabasco

1   cup white wine vinegar
1   small onion, chopped
1   cup salad oil
3   tablespoons papaya seeds

In a blender or food processor, blend the sugar, salt, mustard, MSG, and Tabasco with
the vinegar. Add the onions and blend until smooth. Slowly add the oil. When blended
add the papaya seeds and process until the seeds are the size of ground pepper. Refrigerate. Yield: 2½ cups

GOLF STATISTICS: The odds for an average player getting a hole-in-one stand at 42,942 to 1.

A WINNER PEAR PECAN BLUE CHEESE SALAD

You need a winner of a salad for tonight's dinner for company,
but you also need to practice with your new driver.

⅓ cup oil
⅓ cup seasoned rice wine vinegar
Dash of lemon juice
2 teaspoons honey
1 teaspoon Dijon mustard
¼ teaspoon garlic salt
¼ teaspoon garlic pepper
1 head romaine or a combination
    romaine and iceberg lettuces, prepared

⅓ cup roasted (roast 10 minutes in a 350
    degree oven) pecans, cut in large
    pieces
⅓ cup crumbled blue cheese
1 large pear, peeled, cored, cut up (toss
    with 1 teaspoon lemon juice to keep
    from darkening)

Mix the oil, rice wine vinegar, lemon juice, honey, mustard, garlic salt, and garlic pepper in a jar. Shake well. Set aside while you go to the driving range. At serving time toss the lettuce, pecans, cheese, and pear with enough dressing to coat. Store any extra dressing in the refrigerator (keeps for 2 weeks). Yield: 6 servings

GOLF ATTIRE: Until Jimmy Demaret, "The Ambassador of Golf", (winner of the Masters in '40, '47, and '50) started wearing colorful clothes, you didn't see much other than gray, black, or white on the golf course.

MAKE AHEAD HOT GERMAN POTATO SALAD

A delicious sweet and sour potato salad.

4 medium potatoes	½ cup vinegar
2 slices bacon, chopped	½ cup water
½ medium onion, chopped	½ cup sugar
1 tablespoon flour	½ teaspoon salt

Wash the potatoes and boil in their skins until easily pierced with a knife. Peel and slice. Fry the bacon until just starting to crisp. Add the onion cooking until it softens. Stir in the flour. Mix the water and vinegar and add to the bacon, stirring to prevent lumps. Add the sugar and salt and simmer until slightly thickened. In a 2-quart baking dish, make several layers alternating the potatoes and sauce. When ready to serve, preheat oven to 350 degrees and bake until hot about 25 minutes, or cover and reheat in the microwave for 2 to 3 minutes. Yield: 6 servings

GOLF QUIZ: What is the "dreaded snowman"?

ANSWER: A "snowman" is a score of 8 on a single hole. Also called a "frosty".

HOLE #4

Birdies and Eagles
(chicken and turkey)

NO SKINS GAME BIRD

A delicious baked chicken that roasts for 3 hours while you play 9 holes.

1   roasting chicken, skinned and trimmed
    of fat by the butcher
   Salt and pepper
½   teaspoon dried thyme
2   carrots

2   onions, cut into eighths
6   garlic cloves, cut in half
½   cup water
1   cup chicken broth

Preheat oven to 400 degrees. Season the chicken with salt, pepper, and thyme. Place on rack in roasting pan, arrange vegetables around the chicken, and add the water and broth. Cover the breast of the chicken with a small piece of aluminum foil. Cover the pan with aluminum foil sealed tightly around the edges. Reduce heat to 300 degrees and bake for 3 hours. Skim fat and purée juices and vegetables from the pan in a blender or food processor and thin if necessary with more chicken broth or water to make a sauce to serve along with the chicken. Yield: 4 to 5 servings

GOLF LUCK: In 1912 an illness prevented Harry Vardon from setting sail for America on . . .the *Titanic*. Two years later he won the British Open, his record sixth Open.

CHICKEN IN THE ROUGH

Tastes like a whole chicken dinner in one dish.

1   package (6 ounces) stuffing mix for chicken with flavor packet
1½ cups hot water
6   boneless skinless chicken fillets
6   slices reduced-fat Swiss cheese

1   can (4 ounces) sliced mushrooms, drained
1   can (10¾ ounces) reduced-fat cream of mushroom soup
¼   cup dry white wine or milk

Preheat oven to 375 degrees. In a 8 x 12-inch baking dish that has been coated with no-stick cooking spray combine the stuffing mix, flavor packet, and water. Arrange the chicken on the stuffing. Top each fillet with a slice of cheese and sprinkle with mushrooms. Mix the soup and wine or milk and spoon over the chicken. Bake uncovered for 35 to 45 minutes until hot and bubbly and chicken is cooked through. Serve with cranberry sauce. Yield: 6 servings

GOLF DISASTERS: Lee Trevino, Jerry Heard, and Bobby Nichols were struck by lightning in 1975 during the Western Open.

47

LADIES' DAY CHICKEN

*You had the best score in your foursome, but now you have
guests coming for dinner. Don't panic!*

3½ pounds chicken parts, skin removed
1 envelope onion soup mix

8 ounces Thousand Island dressing
1 jar (12 ounces) apricot preserves

Preheat oven to 350 degrees. Place the chicken in a baking dish that has been sprayed with no-stick cooking spray. Sprinkle soup mix evenly over the chicken, pour dressing over the top, and place a spoonful of the preserves on each piece of chicken. Cover and bake for 1½ hours. Take a shower and change. Serve with quick-cooking rice or small potatoes that you baked at the same time and a tossed green salad. Yield: 4 to 6 servings

GOLF QUOTATION: "Do your best, one shot at a time, and then move on. Remember that golf is just a game."

Nancy Lopez

SCRATCH GOLF GLAZED CHICKEN AND POTATOES

The gourmet in your group is coming for dinner—surprise her with this one.

3 pounds chicken parts
4 medium red potatoes, quartered
1 can (12¾ ounces) golden mushroom
    soup
¼ cup sherry

⅛ teaspoon saffron
    (expensive, but
    essential to the recipe)
¼ cup diced roasted red
    peppers or pimento

Preheat oven to 400 degrees. Place chicken and potatoes in a shallow roasting pan that has been sprayed with no-stick cooking spray. Bake for 45 minutes. Combine rest of ingredients and pour over chicken. Bake 15 minutes longer. Yield: 4 servings

GOLF QUOTATION: "I didn't want to be a millionaire. I just wanted to live like one." Walter Hagen, a golf great, on his luxurious lifestyle.

MULLIGAN MEXICAN CHICKEN

Ten minutes of preparation and 1 hour to bake this delicious south of the border dish.

1   can (30 ounces) fat-free refried beans
1   bell pepper, sliced
1   jalapeño, seeded and chopped fine
3   pounds chicken parts, skin removed

1   envelope taco seasoning mix
1   cup shredded reduced-fat Jack cheese
1   can (15 ounces) tomato sauce
    Chopped cilantro

Preheat oven to 375 degrees. Coat a baking dish with no-stick cooking spray and spread the beans in the bottom of the dish. Arrange the peppers and chicken on the beans and sprinkle with the taco seasoning mix. Sprinkle half of the cheese on the chicken and spoon the tomato sauce over the chicken and cheese. Top with the rest of the cheese. Bake for 1 hour until the chicken is no longer pink and the juices run clear. Garnish with cilantro. Yield: 4 servings

GOLF EQUIPMENT: Standard driver length has quietly gone from 43½ inches to 44 and may soon reach 45. Every inch of club length results in an average gain of 3.2 yards, but a decrease in accuracy of 1.4%.

CHIP AND CRUNCH CHICKEN

Ten minutes preparation and 30 minutes cooking time; your kids will love this!

1½ pounds boneless skinless chicken, cut into bite-size pieces
1 tablespoon butter
1 can (10¾ ounces) reduced-fat cream of mushroom soup
1 cup nonfat milk
½ teaspoon salt
3 cups crushed potato chips
¼ cup shredded reduced-fat sharp cheddar cheese
Paprika

Preheat oven to 350 degrees. Sauté the chicken in the butter until white. Add the soup, milk, and salt. Heat to boiling. Spread ½ the potato chips in the bottom of a greased 2-quart casserole. Spoon the chicken mixture over the chips. Cover with remaining chips. Sprinkle with cheese and paprika. Bake 25 to 30 minutes until hot and bubbly. Serve with cranberry sauce and steamed broccoli. Yield: 6 servings

G⊙LF TRIVIA: What was Tiger Woods' former name?

ANSWER: Eldrick

LA QUINTA PIÑATA CHICKEN

While you watch the Skins Game, these spicy Mexican-style chicken thighs are baking.

2½ cups crushed tortilla chips
1 package taco seasoning mix

6 chicken thighs, skin removed
Juice of 1 lime

Preheat oven to 350 degrees. Mix the crushed chips and the taco seasoning mix in a plastic bag. Moisten the chicken pieces with the lime juice and shake a few at a time in the bag to coat with the chips. Place on a baking sheet that has been coated with no-stick cooking spray. Bake uncovered for 45 minutes until crispy and done. Serve with fruit salsa for dipping. Yield: 4 to 6 servings

GOLF CHRONOLOGY: In 1457, 1471, and 1481 the Scottish parliament forbids golf and football because they hinder military training.

PECAN-CRUSTED DRIVER DRUMSTICKS

Don't practice your swing with these!

1   cup finely chopped pecans
½   cup flour
½   cup cornmeal
½   teaspoon garlic powder

12 Big Betsy-size chicken drum-
      sticks, skin removed
1   cup buttermilk
¼   cup butter, melted
      Salt and pepper

Preheat oven to 400 degrees. Spray a baking sheet with no-stick cooking spray. Combine the nuts, flour, cornmeal, and garlic powder. Dip the drumsticks in the buttermilk and roll in the nut mixture to coat. Arrange the chicken on the baking sheet, bake for 15 minutes, turn, drizzle with butter, season with salt and pepper, and bake for 20 to 30 minutes more until crispy and cooked through. Yield: 12 drumsticks

GOLF RULES: Rule 6-5 states each player should put an identification mark on his ball.

PAR FOR THE COURSE CHICKEN LEGS PAPRIKA

You watched your grandkids play a junior tournament—now they're coming for dinner.

2 tablespoons butter	Paprika
12 chicken drumsticks	Salt and pepper

Preheat oven to 350 degrees. In a shallow roasting pan melt the butter in the oven. Remove the pan from the oven and place the drumsticks in the melted butter. Bake for 50 minutes. Turn the chicken over and baste with the pan drippings. Sprinkle with paprika, salt, and pepper. Bake for 20 minutes longer until the chicken is done and juices run clear. Serve with prepared tater tots and fruit salad. Yield: 4 servings

GOLF RULES: If a ball drops into a hole and is forced out by a jumping frog, has the golfer holed out?

ANSWER: Yes, as soon as the ball was within the circumference of the hole and all of it below the level lip of the hole.

CHIP SHOT CHICKEN

1   package chicken thighs (5 to 6), skin
     removed

1   medium-size bag barbecued potato chips
     (crush enough to make 2 cups crumbs)
1   cup nonfat sour cream

Preheat oven to 350 degrees. Tear a small hole in the chip bag to let the air out. Crush the chips in the bag with a rolling pin. Dip the chicken in the sour cream and roll in the potato chip crumbs. Place on a baking sheet and bake uncovered for 1 hour. Yield: 4 to 6 servings

GOLF QUOTE: Sam Snead once said to Ted Williams, "In golf you have to play your foul balls."

NO SPIKES ALLOWED BAKED CHICKEN

Better than any packaged chicken baking mix and just as fast!

1 package dry onion soup mix
⅔ cup dry bread crumbs

1 egg, beaten with 2 tablespoons milk
12 boneless skinless chicken thighs

Preheat oven to 400 degrees. With a rolling pin or mallet crush the onion soup mix in the envelope. Combine it with the bread crumbs in a pie plate. Put the egg in another pie plate. Dip the chicken in the egg and then coat with the crumbs. Place on a baking dish that has been sprayed with no-stick cooking spray. Bake for 30 minutes or until chicken is no longer pink. Yield: 6 servings

GOLF QUOTATION: Jack Nicklaus was asked why he teed the ball so high. He replied, "After years of experience, I have found that air offers less resistance than dirt."

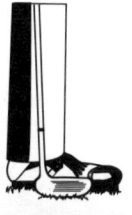

DOUBLE EAGLE TURKEY TIJUANA

Ready in 25 minutes or less, a fun Mexican-style dinner.

1   pound ground turkey
1   tablespoon oil
1½ cups salsa
1   can (15 ounces) black beans, drained
1   can (15 ounces) whole kernel corn,
       drained

1   tomato, chopped
1   bag corn chips
     Shredded cheddar cheese,
       chopped cilantro, guacamole,
       sour cream

In a large nonstick skillet cook the turkey in the oil until no longer pink. Add the salsa, beans, corn, and tomato. Bring to a boil, reduce heat, and simmer for 5 minutes. For each serving place some corn chips in a bowl, top with meat mixture, and sprinkle with cheese and cilantro. Pass the guacamole and sour cream. Yield: 4 to 6 servings

GOLF BROTHER AND SISTER: In the 1920's Joyce Wethered won four British Women's Amateurs and her brother, Roger, won a British Amateur and finished second in a British Open.

EASY EAGLE SCALOPPINE

Turkey cutlets in an Italian sauce that is too delicious to be so easy.

4	turkey cutlets	¼	cup olive oil
½	cup flour	1	can (4 ounces) mushrooms, drained
2	eggs, beaten until frothy	1	package spaghetti sauce mix
½	cup dry bread crumbs	1	cup chicken broth
½	cup grated Parmesan cheese	½	cup dry white wine

Preheat oven to 350 degrees. Dip the cutlets in the flour, then in the egg, and then in a mixture of bread crumbs and Parmesan cheese. Sauté in the oil until golden brown. Place in a shallow baking dish coated with no-stick cooking spray. Mix the mushrooms, spaghetti sauce mix, chicken broth, and wine. Pour over the turkey and bake covered for 30 minutes until turkey is no longer pink inside. Yield: 4 servings

GOLF TRIVIA: How old was the 1997 Connecticut State Women's Amateur golf champion, Elizabeth Janangelo?

TOURNAMENT TURKEY AND RAVIOLI

A delicious low calorie dish ready in 30 minutes.
Use a food processor to quickly chop the vegetables.

1   garlic clove, minced
1   each onion, carrot, stalk celery,
       chopped fine
1   tablespoon olive oil
1   pound ground turkey
1   tablespoon flour, preferably quick-
       mixing
½   cup white wine

1   cup chicken broth
½   teaspoon ground sage
4   shakes Tabasco
½   teaspoon salt
2   packages (13 ounces each) refrigerated
       cheese ravioli, cooked according to
       package directions
    Grated Parmesan cheese

In a nonstick skillet over medium low heat sauté the garlic, onion, carrot, and celery in the oil until soft. Add the turkey and cook until it turns white. Add the flour and stir until it is absorbed. Add the wine, chicken broth, sage, Tabasco, and salt. Cook until thickened. Serve over ravioli. Sprinkle with cheese. Yield: 6 servings

G⊙LF SLANG: What is an "Alice"?

ANSWER: A shot that is hit too timidly and doesn't reach the intended target.

PIN HIGH EASY BAKED TURKEY

You invited the club pro over for dinner.
Maybe you'll get a few free golf tips.

1	half turkey breast or whole turkey thigh (2 to 3 pounds)	½	teaspoon powdered sage
2	tablespoons soft butter	½	teaspoon salt
		⅛	teaspoon pepper

Preheat oven to 350 degrees. Pat the turkey dry with paper towels. Mix the butter, sage, salt, and pepper to a paste. Spread over the skin of the turkey. Place the turkey on a sheet of heavy aluminum foil. Bring the edges up and fold over twice. Do the same with the ends. Place foil-wrapped turkey in a shallow baking pan and bake for 2 hours. Slice the meat and serve with juices, instant mashed potatoes, and cranberry sauce. Yield: 6 servings

GOLF EQUIPMENT: Gene Sarazen is credited with inventing the sand wedge in 1931, but MacGregor came out with it's Scooper wedge at approximately the same time.

HOLE #5

The Hook and Sandtrap
(fish and shellfish)

FAIRWAY FISH IN LEMON DILL SAUCE

1	pound fish fillets	1	teaspoon dill weed
3	tablespoons butter	¼	teaspoon salt
1	tablespoon lemon juice	1	medium green onion, thinly sliced

In a nonstick skillet over medium low heat brown the fillets on both sides in the butter. Add the rest of the ingredients, cover, and cook until the fish flakes easily about 5 minutes longer. Transfer to a serving dish and pour any remaining sauce over the fillets. Yield: 4 servings

GOLF QUOTATION: "You know, it's truly amazing. The more I practice, the luckier I get."

Gary Player

KNOCK DOWN RED SNAPPER

*A good company dish that takes less than 30 minutes. Serve with rice pilaf,
steamed asparagus, and a salad. Voilà! Dinner!*

4	tablespoons butter	1	tablespoon minced onion
1	tablespoon chopped fresh dill or 1 teaspoon dried	1½	pounds red snapper
		⅓	cup grated Parmesan cheese

Preheat oven to 400 degrees. Melt the butter with the dill and onion in a baking dish in the oven (1 to 2 minutes). Add the fish, turning to coat with the herb butter. Bake for 15 minutes. Baste with pan drippings. Sprinkle with the Parmesan cheese and broil for 3 to 5 minutes until crusty on top. Yield: 4 to 6 servings

GOLF RULES: Rule 13-2 forbids moving, bending, or breaking anything growing in the line of play.

OLD COURSE ST. ANDREWS SALMON

Prepare some instant rice and frozen peas and dinner is ready as quick as a golf swing.

4	salmon steaks, ¾-inch thick		Curry Powder
	Juice of 1 lime	2	tablespoons oil
	Salt		

Season the salmon on both sides with the lime, salt, and a generous amount of curry powder. Heat the oil in a large skillet over medium heat. Place the salmon in the oil and quickly cover. Cook 7 to 10 minutes until fork tender. Do not turn. To serve turn with a spatula and serve bottom side up. Yield: 4 servings

GOLF TRAVEL: The island of Phuket, off Thailand's southern coast, is the home of the Blue Canyon Country Club. This course is regarded as the "Augusta National" of Asia and includes one of the first "island" holes in the region.

PERFECT LIE SCALLOPS

A 5 minute recipe with a spicy Caribbean flavor.

2 teaspoons cinnamon	2 teaspoons sugar
2 teaspoons paprika	2 teaspoons ground coriander
1 teaspoon cayenne	1¼ pounds large sea scallops
1 teaspoon salt	1 tablespoon oil

Mix the cinnamon, paprika, cayenne, salt, sugar, and coriander. Remove the little white hinges from the scallops if they haven't already been removed. Rub the spice mixture on both sides of the scallops. Sear the scallops in the oil in a nonstick skillet over medium high heat about 1 minute on each side. Transfer to a serving dish and drizzle any juices over them. Delicious over couscous. Yield: 4 servings

G○LF TRIVIA: Who was the youngest player to win the Master's tournament in Augusta?

ANSWER: Tiger Woods in 1997

SNACK SHOP FISH AND CHIPS

The golf club snack shop serves a great fish and chips. You'd like to duplicate it at home. Put some frozen French fries in the oven before you start. This simple, but delicious recipe takes about 10 minutes.

2 eggs, slightly beaten	1 teaspoon salt
¼ cup milk	⅛ teaspoon pepper
1 cup flour	1½ pounds cod fillets, cut into serving
1 teaspoon paprika	pieces
1 teaspoon dried thyme	3 tablespoons oil

In a pie plate combine the eggs and milk. On a piece of wax paper combine the flour, paprika, thyme, salt, and pepper. Dip the fillets in the egg and then in the flour mixture. Fry in a large skillet in the oil over medium high heat for 2 to 3 minutes per side or until the fish flakes easily. Serve with French fries and malt vinegar. Yield: 4 to 6 servings

GOLF TRIVIA: Which clubs are named after a German cannon which could fire shells miles further than any other?

ANSWER: Callaway's Big Bertha

SLOW PLAY—FAST LINGUINE WITH CLAMS

Your game took longer than you thought. Now you need a speedy recipe.

4   garlic cloves, minced
2   tablespoons olive oil
2   cans (8 ounces each) tomato sauce
1   can (6 ounces) tomato paste
1   teaspoon salt
¼   teaspoon red pepper flakes

¼   cup water
1   tablespoon parsley flakes
2   cans (6½ ounces each) minced or
    chopped clams, drained, reserve juice
1   pound linguine, cooked according to
    package directions

In a medium saucepan sauté the garlic in the oil over low heat until soft. Add the tomato sauce, tomato paste, salt, red pepper, reserved clam juice, water, and parsley and simmer covered for 10 minutes. Add the clams and simmer just long enough to heat through. Transfer the linguine to a pretty pasta bowl and spoon on the sauce. Yield: 4 to 5 servings

G○LF TRIVIA: In what year was the first television coverage of the U.S. Open?

ANSWER: 1947

SHOTGUN START SHRIMP

Luscious shrimp in a creamy cheese sauce to put over rice or pasta.

6	ounces blue cheese, Gorgonzola, or Roquefort	1	tablespoon chopped chives
8	ounces cream cheese	1	garlic clove, chopped
1	tablespoon chopped parsley	¾	cup dry white wine
		2	pounds cleaned raw shrimp

Preheat oven to 400 degrees. In a blender or food processor blend all the ingredients except the shrimp. Arrange the shrimp in a casserole that has been sprayed with no-stick cooking spray. Pour the cheese sauce over the shrimp. Cover and bake for 30 minutes. Yield: 6 servings

GOLF QUIZ: What is a "barky"?

SEMI-FINAL SPICY SHRIMP

So fast and easy. Serve as an appetizer or on a bed of rice as a main dish.

24 large prawns
4   jalapeños, seeded and each sliced
    into 6 thin strips

8   slices lean bacon, each sliced into
    3 pieces
8   bamboo skewers soaked in water
    Barbecue sauce

Shell and devein the shrimp and slice nearly in half. Stuff each shrimp with a slice of jalapeño and wrap with bacon. Skewer 6 shrimp on each bamboo skewer, skewer another bamboo through the shrimp about ½-inch from the first (to make it easier to turn), and grill or broil, basting with the barbecue sauce. Yield: 4 large servings

GOLF HISTORY: President Eisenhower played a presidential record 100 rounds of golf in one year.

The HOOK and the SANDTRAP

SKINS GAME SHRIMP

*This saucy shrimp takes but minutes. The frozen puff pastry shells
bake for 25 minutes while you set the table.*

4	frozen puff pastry shells	1	cup peas (canned or frozen, thawed)
1	can (10¾ ounces) cream of shrimp soup	2	tablespoons chopped pimento or
¼	cup milk		roasted red peppers
¾	pound small cooked shrimp		Salt and pepper

Preheat oven to 400 degrees. Bake the puff pastry shells according to package directions.
In a medium saucepan heat the soup and milk. Add the shrimp, peas and pimento or red
pepper stirring until well blended and warm through. Do not boil. Season with salt and
pepper. Serve over the baked pastry shells. Yield: 4 servings

GOLF HAZARD: At the Bali Golf and Country Club in the resort of Nusa Dua,
holes 10 through 16 plunge into a lush coconut grove where some palms are
as high as 100 feet making falling coconuts a hazard if you stray
from the course.

THE CADDIE'S SHRIMP CREOLE

The caddie was from the deep South and gave you his golfing mother's quickie recipe.

2 cans (16 ounces each) stewed tomatoes
¾ pound cooked salad shrimp
2 teaspoons minced dried onion
½ teaspoon salt

¼ teaspoon Tabasco
½ teaspoon dried thyme
1 tablespoon flour in
    2 tablespoons water

Heat the tomatoes, add the rest of the ingredients, cover, and cook 5 minutes until heated through and slightly thickened. Serve over instant rice. Yield: 4 to 6 servings

GOLF RULES: If a player in a fit of frustration hits his club on a tree and breaks it, can he send for a replacement?

ANSWER: No, because it was not broken in the normal course of play.

BUCKET OF CRAB

A fast seafood dinner for days you spend too much time hitting a bucket of balls.

1 can (14 ounces) chicken broth
¾ cup dry white wine (save the rest for dinner)
2 tablespoons butter
2 tablespoons chopped parsley
1 teaspoon dried thyme
1 tablespoon soy sauce

1 tablespoon lemon juice
1 tablespoon crushed garlic
2 cooked Dungeness crabs, cleaned and cracked (shell and gills removed; claws twisted off body and cracked; body cut into quarters)—the fish monger will be happy to do this for you

In a large pot heat everything but the crab to boiling. Add the crab, lower the heat, and simmer for 4 to 5 minutes until crab is hot. Serve crab and broth in wide soup bowls with crusty bread to soak up the broth. Yield: 2 to 4 servings

GOLF HEALTH: Several companies are making sun-protective sportswear that blocks more than 97% of the sun's harmful rays.

HOLE #6

The Shank and the Links
(meat and sausage)

PRO SHOP PORK CHOPS AND CREAMY GRAVY

You spent too long browsing in the pro shop. No problem, dinner is only minutes away.

¼ cup plus 2 tablespoons
   quick-mixing flour
½ teaspoon garlic salt
¼ teaspoon pepper
½ teaspoon ground sage or
   poultry seasoning

2 tablespoons plus 1½ cups milk
4 boneless center cut pork chops,
   ½-inch thick
2 tablespoons oil

Mix the ¼ cup flour, salt, and pepper in a pie plate. In another plate dip the pork chops in the 2 tablespoons milk, then into the flour to coat. In a nonstick skillet over medium high heat brown the chops in the oil on one side (2 to 3 minutes). Turn the chops, add the 2 tablespoons flour, sage, and 1½ cups milk. Reduce the heat to low and simmer stirring until the gravy thickens and pork chops are done about 4 minutes. Yield: 4 servings

GOLF HISTORY: Babe Zaharias, who died of cancer at 41, was not the greatest woman golfer, but possibly the greatest athlete. In the 1932 Olympics she won the 80 meters hurdles, the javelin, and came second in the high jump.

"DRIVE FOR SHOW 'N PUTT FOR DOUGH"
PORK CHOPS 'N WILD RICE

1   box (6 ounces) long grain and
    wild rice mix
1   can (10¾ ounces) cream of
    mushroom soup

1   can (4 ounces) mushrooms, drained
1¾ cups water
4   pork chops
    Paprika

Preheat oven to 350 degrees. Combine the uncooked rice and flavor packet, soup, mushrooms, and water in a 11 x 7- or 8 x 8-inch baking dish. Arrange the pork chops on top and sprinkle with the paprika. Bake for 1½ hours or until chops are brown and rice is tender. Yield: 4 servings

GOLF HIGHLIGHTS: In 1973 Jack Nicklaus was PGA Player of the Year and was the first man in golf to win over $2 million.

PINNACLE PORK CHOPS WITH TEQUILA

4 center cut loin pork chops
2 tablespoons jalapeño or red pepper
   jelly, melted
2 tablespoons tequila

2 tablespoons lime juice
½ teaspoon salt
⅛ teaspoon pepper

Combine all the ingredients in a plastic bag and marinate 8 hours in the refrigerator while you go to the golf course. Grill or broil, basting with the marinade 7 minutes on each side or until pork is cooked. Serve with refried black beans from a can and slices of fresh or frozen mango. Yield: 4 servings

GOLF INFLATION: In 1953 the greens fee at Pebble Beach was $5. In October 1997 the greens fee went up to $350.

PRO-AM PORK CHOPS WITH BEER

In less than 30 minutes tasty and beautiful pork chops studded with seeds.

4	loin pork chops	2	tablespoons oil
2	garlic cloves, crushed	1	cup beer
¼	teaspoon pepper	1	beef bouillon cube
1	tablespoon caraway seeds	1	tablespoon prepared mustard
2	tablespoons flour		

Rub each chop with the garlic and pepper. Press the caraway seeds onto the chops. Dredge the chops in the flour and brown on both sides in the oil. Remove from the pan and keep warm by covering with foil. Add the beer, bouillon cube, and mustard to the pan stirring to dissolve the bouillon cube. Simmer until slightly thickened. Return the chops to the pan and simmer covered 10 to 15 minutes. Transfer chops to a serving platter and pour juices over the pork. Yield: 4 servings

GOLF PROTÉGÉ: Tiger Woods first beat his father at golf at age 11, shooting a 71 to Earl's 72 at the Navy course at Los Alamitos.

BACKSWING BEAN CURD

*Chopped ginger and garlic can be purchased in small jars
to make this quick dish even quicker.*

16 ounces firm tofu
2 tablespoons chopped ginger
1 teaspoon chopped garlic
8 ounces lean ground pork
2 teaspoons sesame oil

1 tablespoon cornstarch
1⅓ cups chicken broth
3 green onions, sliced
1-2 teaspoons Chinese chili paste
2 tablespoons soy sauce

Drain the tofu, pat dry with paper towels, and cut into ½-inch squares. Sauté the ginger, garlic, and pork in the oil. Stir the cornstarch into the chicken broth and add to the meat mixture along with the green onions, chili paste, soy sauce, and tofu and cook over low heat for about 8 minutes. Serve over quick rice. Yield: 4 servings

GOLF TRAVEL: In 1997 *Golf For Women Magazine* ranked the Wailea Golf Club in Hawaii as the country's third most women-friendly course.

WINNING STREAK HAM LOAVES

A delicious way to use leftover ham.

1 pound lean ham, ground in food
processor or by the butcher
½ pound lean pork, ground in food
processor or by the butcher
½ cup milk

1 egg, beaten
1 teaspoon spicy brown mustard
1 cup bread crumbs
Chinese sweet and sour sauce

Preheat oven to 350 degrees. Combine the ham, pork, milk, egg, mustard, and bread crumbs. Shape into 4 loaves of equal size. Place in a shallow baking dish and coat with the sweet and sour sauce. Bake for 1 hour. Serve with sweet potatoes that baked at the same time. Yield: 4 servings

GOLF GREATS: In 1965 Sam Snead won the Greater Greensboro open at the age of 52. As of 1997 he remains the oldest winner of a regular PGA event. In 1937 newspapers in Scotland, reporting on the Ryder Cup Matches in Southport, England, printed his picture and called him "The Big Bertha of Golf" because of the length of his tee shots.

WAILEA KALUA PORK AND SWEET POTATOES

*You can pretend you've just finished playing Wailea Golf Club's
championship Emerald Course and are dining under the palm trees.*

4-6 pounds pork butt
2 teaspoons salt
1 tablespoon minced ginger (see note)

¾ teaspoon minced garlic
Few drops of liquid smoke
6 sweet potatoes, scrubbed

Preheat oven to 325 degrees. Remove excess fat from pork and make slashes with a sharp knife over the surface. Mix the salt, ginger, garlic, and liquid smoke and rub over the pork. Wrap the pork in heavy duty aluminum foil and seal the edges well. Place in a shallow roasting pan and bake for 6 hours. Put the sweet potatoes in the oven for the last 2 hours the pork is baking. Yield: 6 to 8 servings

Note: The grocery stores carry small jars of minced ginger and garlic.

GOLF TRIVIA: How many dimples are there on a Wilson Stagg Titanium Distance 90 golf ball?

ANSWER: 500

JUNIOR GOLF POLISH SAUSAGE AND RICE

The kids from Junior Golf Camp are coming for dinner—
maybe I'd better double this recipe!

1   can (28 ounces) crushed tomatoes with
         added purée
½   cup chopped bell pepper
¾   pound Polish sausage, sliced into
         ½-inch slices

1½   teaspoons basil
2   cups instant rice
¾   cup shredded mozzarella cheese

In a large skillet or Dutch oven heat the tomatoes, bell pepper, sausage, and basil to boiling. Stir in rice, cover pan, and remove from heat. Let stand 10 minutes until rice is tender. Fluff with a fork. Sprinkle the cheese on top, cover, and cook on low until cheese melts about 5 minutes. Yield: 4 to 5 servings

GOLF READING: Sam Snead's *The Game I Love: Wisdom, Insight, and Instruction from Golf's Greatest Player.*

81

BOGEY BRATWURST IN BEER

Serve your friends "brats and beer" while you watch the Ryder Cup on television.

2	pounds bratwurst	1	teaspoon peppercorns
1	can beer	1	teaspoon mustard seeds

Simmer the bratwurst, beer, peppercorns, and mustard seeds uncovered for 20 minutes. Remove the bratwurst and grill until lightly brown. Serve on crusty rolls with Make Ahead Hot German Potato Salad, recipe in Hole (chapter) #3 and cold German beer. Yield: 6 servings

G○LF QUIZ: How many players are on each team in the Ryder Cup?

DON'T SHANK IT LAMB SHANKS

4   lean lamb shanks
    Salt and pepper
1   tablespoon oil

1½ cups strong coffee
1   cup bourbon

Preheat oven to 275 degrees. Salt and pepper the lamb shanks and brown in the oil over medium-high heat for 5 minutes. Put in a Dutch oven and pour over the coffee and bourbon. Bake for one round of golf (5 to 6 hours). Degrease the sauce remaining in the pan and serve on the side. Yield: 4 servings

GOLF PARTNERS: "Alternate Shot" used to be popular in couples golf under the name of "Scotch Foursome". It disappeared and then resurfaced in Ryder Cup matches. In the alternate shot format each player on a 2-player team takes turns hitting one ball until that ball is holed out. The score on each hole is the total number of shots taken by both players on that hole.

WOMEN'S U.S. OPEN CROCKPOT MEAT LOAF

The Women's U.S. Open is on television.
Put the meat in the slow cooker and don't miss a single shot.

2 pounds extra lean ground beef
2 envelopes Sloppy Joe seasoning mix
2 eggs, beaten
¼ cup catsup
1 minced onion or 2 tablespoons minced dried onion

1 small bell pepper, finely chopped
1 cup oatmeal
2 cans (8 ounces each) tomato sauce
4 teaspoons sugar
Several dashes of Tabasco

Mix the beef, seasoning mix, eggs, catsup, onion, bell pepper, and oatmeal and form a loaf in the bottom of your crockpot. Mix the tomato sauce, sugar, and Tabasco and pour over the loaf. Cover and cook on low for 8 to 10 hours. Yield: 6 to 8 servings

GOLF BETS: 36% of men golfers say they play with a bet on the line, but only 10% of women.

"TIME FOR 9 HOLES" BEEF CHILI POTATOES

Bake potatoes in your crockpot while you play golf.
Put together a hearty topping in 15 minutes.

4   baking potatoes
1   pound extra lean ground beef
1   tablespoon chili powder
½   teaspoon salt
1   can (15 ounces) spicy chili beans

1   cup plus ½ cup grated reduced-fat
    sharp cheddar cheese
¼   cup sliced green onions or chopped
    yellow onion

Prick the potatoes with a fork and wrap in foil. Place in a crockpot. Cover and cook on high for 2½ to 4 hours or on low for 6 to 8 hours. Grab your sticks and beat it to the golf course. Fifteen minutes before dinner, brown the ground beef in a large skillet over medium-high heat, breaking it up with a large spoon. Stir in the chili powder, salt, beans, and 1 cup cheese. Cook and stir until heated through. Remove the potatoes from the crockpot, cut a slit in the top of the potatoes, fluff with a fork, and spoon the beef mixture over each potato. Top with remaining cheese and onions. Yield: 4 servings

GOLF TRAVEL: Alabama has perhaps the most affordable golf in the world. The Robert Jones Golf Trail has 7 public facilities up and down the state with green fees of $49 or less.

The SHANK and the LINKS

SANDBAGGER STEAK

For the man in your life.

3   beef bouillon cubes, crushed
1   teaspoon crushed garlic
2   tablespoons red wine
1   tablespoon Dijon mustard

4   beef loin or rib eye steaks, cut
    ¾-inch thick
1   tablespoon butter
⅓   cup water

Mix the bouillon, garlic, wine, and mustard and spread on both sides of each steak. Fry the steaks in a large nonstick skillet in the butter over medium high heat 8 to 10 minutes for rare or until desired doneness. Remove steaks to serving platter, add water to the hot pan scraping up any brown bits of flavoring and pour this pan gravy over the steaks before serving. Yield: 4 steaks

GOLF TRIVIA: Tiger Woods was named after whom?

ANSWER: Col. Tiger Phong, a Vietnamese soldier and battlefield friend of Tiger Woods' father. He died September 9, 1976 in a communist prison camp.

LUCKY BOUNCE BEEF AND GREEN PEPPERS

This version of green pepper steak is so easy it's like a lucky bounce.
Serve over steamed rice.

1¾ cup hot water
2 beef bouillon cubes
2 tablespoons cornstarch
4 tablespoons soy sauce
3 tablespoons brown sugar
½ teaspoon red pepper flakes or
   Chinese chili paste

1 pound flank steak, sliced diagonally
   into ¼-inch strips
2 tablespoons oil
2 bell peppers, cut into thin strips
   1-inch long

Combine the water, bouillon, cornstarch, soy sauce, sugar, and red pepper or chili paste in a small bowl and mix well. Brown the meat in the oil over high heat. Add the bouillon mixture and stir until thickened. Stir in the green pepper, cover, and cook until pepper is crisp-tender about 5 minutes. Yield: 4 servings

GOLF TRIVIA: In 1997, according to a J.D. Powers and Associates survey, 52 % of Porsche drivers were golfers, compared to 46 % of BMW drivers and 34% of Saab drivers.

THE EQUALIZER SHORT RIBS

These flavorful ribs are so tender they almost fall off the bone. Men will love this.

6 large beef short ribs
1 tablespoon season salt
1 teaspoon garlic powder

2 teaspoons Italian herb seasoning
1 cup red wine

Preheat oven to 325 degrees. Put the ribs, fat side up, in a shallow baking pan. Combine the rest of the ingredients and pour over the ribs. Bake uncovered for 2½ hours turning once or twice (optional). Serve with buttered noodles and a salad. Yield: 6 servings

GOLF EQUIPMENT: In 1991 Callaway introduces "Big Bertha". By 1997 no one on the PGA tour uses a wooden driver.

WORLD CUP COLA ROAST BEEF

What could be easier? Put this in the oven and try to break 90 today.

1   (4 to 4½ pound) beef roast,
      trimmed of fat

1   package dry onion soup mix
1   can (12 ounces) regular cola

Preheat oven to 300 degrees. Put the roast in a baking pan. Sprinkle with the onion soup. Pour the cola into the pan. Cover very tightly with aluminum foil or a lid. Roast for 4 to 4½ hours until tender. Thicken gravy if needed with 1 tablespoon cornstarch in 2 tablespoons water. Yield: 6 to 8 servings

GOLF ODDITY: Phil Mickelson, a member of America's 1997 Ryder Cup Team, plays golf left-handed although he is a right-hander in all other things. As a child he learned to play golf by mirroring his father's right-handed stroke.

EASY SHOT ROAST BEEF WITH GRAVY

You can use a less tender cut of beef (cross-rib, round, or rump)
for this slow cooked roast that produces a wonderful gravy.

1   (3 to 4 pound) beef roast, trimmed of
    fat
1   tablespoon oil
1   can (10¾ ounces) reduced-fat cream of
    mushroom soup

1   package dry onion soup mix
¼   cup steak sauce
⅓   cup water

Preheat oven to 300 degrees. Brown the meat in the oil on all sides. Put in roasting pan. Mix the mushroom soup, onion soup, steak sauce, and water and pour over the beef. Cover with lid or foil and bake for 4 hours. Yield: 6 to 8 servings.

GOLF WINNINGS: When the first Skins game was played in 1983, Tom Lehman had just completed his first year on the PGA Tour. His total winnings for the year were $9,413. In 1997 he made $300,000 for playing 18 holes in the Skins game.

"TIME TO GET IN A QUICK ROUND" BEEF

1   package dry onion soup mix
2   cans (4 ounces each) mushrooms, undrained

2   tablespoons steak sauce
3   pounds beef chuck, cut into 1½-inch cubes

Line a shallow pan with heavy duty aluminum foil, leaving enough on the ends so that it can be sealed over the meat. Mix the onion soup with the juice from the mushrooms and the steak sauce. Spray the foil with no-stick cooking spray. Pour half of the sauce on the foil, add the beef, and top with the rest of the sauce. Add the mushrooms. Seal the foil tightly. Bake in a 275 degree oven for 5 hours. Serve over rice or noodles. Yield: 6 to 8 servings

GOLF TRIVIA: Which course has a floating green?

ANSWER: The 14th hole at the Coeur d' Alene Club in Idaho is a floating green made of expanded polysty-rene surrounded by water.

7 HOUR OR GOLFER'S MIRACLE ROAST

Put this in the oven and spend the day golfing.

1   boneless chuck roast, (4½ to 6 pounds),   Salt and pepper
     trimmed of excess fat, rolled, and tied

Preheat oven to 200 degrees. Let the roast come to room temperature if possible. Place in a shallow roasting pan (one with sides not more than 3-inches), fat side up. Salt and pepper the meat. Roast for 7 hours without opening the oven door. It can even go 1 hour more or longer. You'll be amazed at this tender and juicy roast. Yield: 8 to 10 servings

GOLF HISTORY: In 1985 when Seve Ballesteros led the Europeans to a stunning upset at the Belfry in England, the Ryder Cup assumed new stature as a major event.

HOLE #7

The Mulligan
(stews, casseroles, and pasta)

NIBLICK 5 HOUR STEW

What do you know? Time for 18 holes.

2 pounds beef stew meat	½ cup dry bread crumbs
2 stalks celery, cut into 2-inch pieces	3 tablespoons minute tapioca
6 carrots, cut into 2-inch pieces	1 tablespoon garlic salt
4 small onions, quartered	1 tablespoon sugar
1 can (8 ounces) tomato sauce	

Preheat oven to 250 degrees. Mix all the ingredients in a casserole or Dutch oven. Cover. Bake for 5 hours without lifting the lid. Yield: 6 servings

GOLF HISTORY: Jack Nicklaus' first professional win came at the 1962 U.S. Open at age 22.

BIG BERTHA BEEF AND ALE STEW

Delicious flavor with a bread crust.

2 tablespoons oil	2 garlic cloves, crushed
1½ pounds chuck or round steak, cut into palm-size squares	1 bay leaf
2 onions, sliced	1 teaspoon salt
1 tablespoon quick-mixing flour	¼ teaspoon pepper
1 pint dark ale or beer	4-6 slices French bread, day-old is good
	Dijon mustard

Preheat oven to 325 degrees. Over high heat in a deep iron frying pan or a Dutch oven brown the meat in the oil on both sides. Lower the heat, add the onions and brown. Dust the meat with the flour. Add the ale or beer, 1 pint water, garlic, bay leaf, salt, and pepper. Bring to a boil. Take off the heat. Cover and bake for 2½ to 3 hours. Forty minutes before serving, spread the bread lightly with the mustard and push down into stew until it is well soaked with gravy. It will bob up again. Continue to bake uncovered until the bread forms a brown crust. Yield: 4 to 6 servings

GOLF SCORING SECRET: For every hour of practice, spend at least 30 minutes on shots inside 100 yards.

"YOU'RE AWAY" VEAL CASSEROLE

(Plenty of time for 9 holes)

1½ pounds veal, cut for stew
½ medium onion, chopped
¼ cup slivered almonds
½ teaspoon rosemary

½ teaspoon marjoram
½ teaspoon garlic powder
1 can (10¾ ounces) cream of
    chicken soup

Preheat oven to 250 degrees. Spray a large shallow casserole with no-stick cooking spray. Put the meat in and sprinkle with the onion, almonds, and herbs. Spread the undiluted soup on top. Bake for 3½ hours. Serve on rice. Yield: 4 servings

GOLF TRAVEL: Traveling golfers are finding it hard to reserve tee times. Many are turning to tee-time reservation services. *Golf Digest's* T-links, Jack Nicklaus' Golden Bear Travel, and Tee-matic on the Internet will book advance tee times.

HANDICAP HAM AND BEANS

2   tablespoons brown sugar
2   tablespoons prepared mustard
2   cans (16 ounces each) pork and
    beans in tomato sauce

1   fully cooked ham slice (about
    1½ pounds) cut into 6 pieces

Preheat oven to 350 degrees. In a small bowl mix the brown sugar and mustard. Spoon the beans into a baking dish that has been coated with no-stick cooking spray. Spread each piece of ham with the sugar/mustard mixture and place on top of the beans. Bake for 35 minutes until ham is heated through and beans are hot and bubbly. Serve with cornbread or beer bread from a mix. Yield: 6 servings

GOLF TRIVIA: Which major player was entertaining President Clinton at his estate when the President fell on the stairs and severely injured his knee?

ANSWER: Greg Norman

The MULLIGAN

VALDERRAMA SPANISH HAM ROLL-UPS

This is a "gimme". These roll-ups are easy to make and taste great.

10 thin ham slices
10 (6-inch) flour tortillas
8 ounces reduced-fat Jack cheese,
   cut into 10 (½-inch) strips

1 can (4 ounces) whole green chiles,
   cut into 10 (¼-inch) strips
1 can (11 ounces) nacho cheese soup
½ cup milk

Preheat oven to 350 degrees. Place 1 slice of ham on each tortilla. Put 1 strip of cheese and 1 strip of chile on the ham. Roll the tortilla up and place seamside down in a 9 x 13-inch pan that has been coated with no-stick cooking spray. Whisk together the soup and the milk and pour over the rolled tortillas. Cover with foil and bake for 45 minutes. Yield: 6 to 12 servings

GOLF APPAREL: The most famous single accessory of the 40's and 50's was the flat white cap worn by Ben Hogan.

ARIZONA'S TROON NORTH TORTILLA CASSEROLE

Like delicious beef and cheese enchiladas, but easier!

1	pound extra lean ground beef	1	package taco seasoning mix
1	medium onion, chopped	6	(9-inch) flour tortillas
1	can (15 ounces) stewed tomatoes	8	ounces reduced-fat cheddar cheese,
1	can (8 ounces) tomato sauce		grated
1	can (4 ounces) diced green chiles		

Preheat oven to 350 degrees. In a large nonstick skillet brown the beef and onions. Add the rest of the ingredients except the tortillas and cheese. Simmer covered 15 minutes. Spread ¼ of the mixture in a 9 x 13-inch baking dish coated with no-stick cooking spray. Top with a layer of 2 tortillas, more meat, and then a layer of cheese. Repeat 2 more times. Bake for 25 minutes until hot and cheese is melted. Yield: 4 to 6 servings

GOLF TRAVEL: The Desert Inn is the only championship course on the entire Las Vegas strip, and *Golf Digest* rates it among the leading 75 golf resorts.

TOUGH DOGLEG, BUT TERRIFIC TAMALE PIE

A very easy tamale pie for hungry golfers.

1   can (15 ounces) chili con carne with or without beans
1   can (15 ounces) black beans or red kidney beans, drained
1   can (15 ounces) whole kernel corn, drained

½   cup pitted ripe olives, sliced
1   can (28 ounces) tamales
¾   cup grated reduced-fat sharp cheddar cheese

Preheat oven to 350 degrees. Spray a shallow 8 x 8-inch baking dish with no-stick cooking spray. Put in the chili, beans, and corn, stirring to mix. Sprinkle with the olives. Arrange the tamales on top (remove the wrappers if there are any and drain any grease). Sprinkle with the cheese. Bake for 30 minutes until hot and bubbly. Yield: 6 servings

GOLF TRAVEL: With nearly 50 golf facilities, Spain's Costa del Sol has exploded as a golfing destination.

CHIP UP CHILI CASSEROLE

This can be put together faster than a U.S. Open green.

1   package (10½ ounces) corn chips,
    crushed in the bag
3   cans (15 ounces each) chili con carne
1   bunch green onions, chopped
1   can (4 ounces) sliced black olives

4   large tomatoes, sliced
    Salt and pepper
1   cup grated sharp cheddar cheese
    Shredded lettuce

Preheat oven to 350 degrees. Put the corn chips in the bottom of a baking dish that has been sprayed with no-stick cooking spray. Cover with the chili con carne. Sprinkle with the onions and olives. Lay tomato slices on the top and sprinkle with salt and pepper if needed. Top with grated cheese. Bake for 30 minutes until hot and bubbly. Garnish with shredded lettuce. Yield: 6 servings

GOLF AVERAGES: The average 18-hole score for a woman golfer is 108.

The MULLIGAN

CADDY SHACK CHILI MAC CASSEROLE

This hearty dish is a favorite at caddy parties.

1 cup macaroni
2 cans (16 ounces) chili with beans
  Dill pickle slices

Chopped onions and shredded
  cheddar cheese

Preheat oven to 375 degrees. Cook the macaroni according to package directions. Drain. Heat the chili and combine with the macaroni in a 1½-quart casserole that has been sprayed with no-stick cooking spray. Top with the pickle slices. Bake for 30 minutes or until hot and bubbly. Garnish with onions and cheese. Serve with garlic bread. Yield: 4 servings

GOLF TRIVIA: Who was the star of the cult golf movie *Caddy Shack*?

"MADE THE CUT" CHILI AND SPAGHETTI

1   pound extra lean ground beef
1   medium onion, chopped
1   garlic clove, minced
2   cans (8 ounces each) tomato sauce
1   cup water
½   ounce unsweetened baking chocolate
1   tablespoon red wine vinegar

1   tablespoon chili powder
1   teaspoon ground allspice
½   teaspoon cinnamon
½   teaspoon salt
1   pound spaghetti cooked according to
     package directions
     Shredded cheddar cheese and chopped
     onions

In a large saucepan brown the meat with the onion and garlic. Add the rest of the ingredients except spaghetti, cheese, and onion. Bring to a boil. Reduce heat and simmer for 30 minutes. Serve over spaghetti. Top with cheese and onions. Yield: 4 servings

GOLF QUOTATION: Steve Jones at the 1997 Canadian Open gave this advice to Canadians who want to be pro golfers, "Move to Arizona."

FAT SHOT FETTUCCINE

*A creamy dish of spinach fettuccine, peas, and ham
that takes about 10 minutes to prepare.*

1 cup chopped ham
1 cup heavy cream
1 package (10 ounces) frozen peas,
  thawed

½ cup plus 2 tablespoons grated
  Parmesan cheese
¼ teaspoon salt
½ teaspoon pepper
12 ounces spinach fettuccine

In a medium saucepan cook the ham until starting to crisp. Add the cream, peas, ½ cup Parmesan cheese, salt, and pepper. Cook for 5 minutes. Do not boil; just heat through. Cook the fettuccine according to package directions. Drain and transfer to a serving platter. Pour the sauce over the noodles. Sprinkle with additional 2 tablespoons Parmesan cheese. Yield: 4 servings

GOLF INTERNATIONAL: Golf courses are springing up in South China. Even at $400,000 a year, they are cheaper than Hong Kong's 6 courses which charge $1.8 million a year.

CART PATH SPAGHETTI CARBONARA

This easy bacon and eggs pasta dish was supposedly invented during World War II to please Americans stationed in Italy.

½ pound bacon, cut into ¼-inch strips
2 tablespoons softened butter
2 eggs, beaten
½ cup plus 2 tablespoons grated
   Parmesan cheese

1 pound spaghetti or fettuccine
Salt
Freshly grated black pepper
   (don't leave out)

Fry the bacon until lightly brown, but not too crisp. Transfer the bacon to a serving bowl with the butter, eggs, and ½ cup Parmesan cheese. Cook the pasta according to package directions and toss the pasta in the bowl with the bacon and egg mixture. The heat of the pasta will cook the eggs. Add salt and pepper to taste. Sprinkle with additional 2 tablespoons cheese. Yield: 4 to 6 servings

G⚬LF HISTORY: During one nine-month period in 1912, three of the greatest golfers the world has ever known were born: Byron Nelson, Sam Snead, and Ben Hogan.

SCORECARD SAUSAGE, PEPPERS, AND SPAGHETTI

3 bell peppers, seeded and cut into large chunks
1-3 tablespoons olive oil
Garlic salt

1 pound hot or mild Italian sausage links
¾ cup red wine
1 pound spaghetti

Preheat oven to 350 degrees. In a cast iron frying pan or a Dutch oven, sauté the peppers in the olive oil until they start to soften. Salt to taste. Remove and set aside. Brown the sausages in the same pan. Add the wine, cover the pan with lid or foil, and bake for 40 minutes. Add the peppers and bake for 30 minutes longer. Cook the spaghetti according to package directions. Place on a serving platter and spoon the sausages and peppers on top. Serve with grated Parmesan or Romano cheese. Yield: 4 servings

GOLF QUIZ: What are the 4 championships that have come to be known as the majors?

ANSWER: Masters, United States Open, British Open, and US PGA.

ON THE GREEN SPAGHETTI

The supermarket produce manager can order the fresh basil for you.
If pine nuts are unavailable, substitute walnuts.

2   cups packed fresh basil leaves
2   garlic cloves, crushed
2   tablespoons pine nuts
½   cup extra virgin olive oil

1   teaspoon salt
½   cup grated Parmesan cheese
2   tablespoons grated Romano cheese
1   pound spaghetti

Combine the basil, garlic, pine nuts, olive oil, salt and cheeses in a food processor or blender and process until basil is finely ground. Cook the spaghetti according to package directions, reserving 1 cup cooking liquid. Toss the pasta with the green sauce. If it is too dry or thick add a little reserved pasta cooking water and toss again. Yield: 6 to 8 servings

GOLF ETIQUETTE: It is imperative that players do not allow their shadows to cross the line of the players who are putting, especially in the early morning and late afternoon when shadows can run the length of the green.

RICOCHET RIGATONI

You drove your ball into the woods. It hit a tree and bounced back onto the fairway. Celebrate your luck with a quick pasta dinner.

¾ pound cauliflower florets, sliced lengthwise into ¼-inch slices	1 tablespoon anchovy paste (do not leave out)
3 tablespoons butter	¼ red bell pepper, thinly sliced
3 tablespoons olive oil	12 ounces rigatoni
2 garlic cloves, minced	¼ cup grated Parmesan cheese Coarsely ground black pepper

Steam the cauliflower until tender. Turn off heat. Remove the cover. In a small saucepan over low heat, simmer the butter, olive oil, garlic, anchovy paste, and bell pepper for about 4 minutes. Cook the rigatoni according to package directions. Toss cauliflower, butter mixture, and cheese with the rigatoni. Sprinkle with the black pepper. Yield: 4 to 6 servings

G◯LF QUOTATION: "Finish high and let 'em fly." Patty Berg

THE GREEN MONSTER MACARONI AND CHEESE

Loved by golfers of all ages.

8 ounces elbow macaroni
¼ cup butter
1 package (8 ounces) process cheddar
    cheese, cut into cubes

½ cup milk
1 beaten egg
1 teaspoon onion salt
⅛ teaspoon pepper

Cook the macaroni according to package directions. Drain and return to the pan. Add remaining ingredients and cook over low heat stirring until the cheese is melted. Yield: 4 to 8 servings

GOLF EQUIPMENT: Until late in the 1920's, when the steel shaft was introduced, clubs with shafts of hickory, ash, or bamboo and wooden or iron heads were the norm.

TOP FLIGHT HUEVOS RANCHEROS

Sunday (golf day) calls for a hearty breakfast.

2	tablespoons minced onion	2	canned jalapeños, minced or
1	garlic clove, minced		2 tablespoons diced green chiles
1	tablespoon oil	1	can (8 ounces) tomato sauce
½	teaspoon oregano		Salt
		4	eggs

In a large frying pan, cook the onion and garlic in the oil over medium low heat until soft. Add the oregano, jalapeños or green chiles, tomato sauce, and salt to taste. Simmer a few minutes. Crack the eggs into the sauce and poach by covering with a lid for 4 to 5 minutes. Serve the eggs with refried beans, warm tortillas, and fried breakfast sausage. Yield: 2 servings

GOLF TIP: When putting you want the speed of the ball to be at its fullest at impact. This means a symmetrical stroke length. If you take the putter back 6 inches, follow through 6 inches.

HOLE #8

The Club and the Slice
(sandwiches, pizza, and bread)

30 MINUTE TEE TIME SOFT TACOS

You'll never miss the meat! Roasting the vegetables brings out great flavor.

6 plum tomatoes	1 can (16 ounces) refried beans
2 small bell peppers	1 package (soft taco size) flour tortillas
2 medium onions	Salsa, guacamole, shredded cheddar
2 tablespoons oil	cheese
1 package taco seasoning mix	

Preheat oven to 475 degrees. Cut the tomatoes, peppers, and onions into ½-inch wedges and toss on a baking sheet with the oil. Sprinkle with the taco seasoning mix. Bake 15 minutes. Warm the beans in the microwave or in a small pan over low heat. Spread 2 tablespoons of refried beans inside each tortilla, fold over. Place on a baking sheet and bake with the vegetables for 2 minutes until the tortillas are warm. Spoon the vegetables on top of the beans. Serve with salsa, guacamole, and cheese. Yield: 10 tacos

G◯LF ADVICE: "I always advise people not to give advice."

P.G. Wodehouse

FLAGSTICK FIESTA QUESADILLAS

Made from scratch (almost) and in less than 30 minutes.

1½ pounds boneless skinless chicken
1 can (11 ounces) nacho cheese soup
8 (8-inch) flour tortillas

½ cup shredded cheddar
  cheese
Salsa

Cover the chicken with water and simmer for 15 minutes. When cool, drain and cut into small pieces. Preheat oven to 400 degrees. Mix the cooked chicken and the soup. Top each tortilla with ¼ cup of the mixture. Moisten the edges of the tortilla with water, fold in half (half-moon shape), and press the edges together. Place on 2 large baking sheets that have been sprayed with no-stick cooking spray and also spray the tops of the tortillas. Sprinkle with the cheese, and bake for 10 minutes until hot. Serve with salsa and Mexican beer. Yield: 4 to 8 servings

GOLF RULES: Decision 24-5 states: "Water visible through undue effort with the feet (stomping) is not casual water."

TROPHY MANGO BEEF WRAPS

A fancy name for a very different meat and tropical fruit burrito.
Make a salad and dinner is ready in 10 minutes.

1   tablespoon plus 1 tablespoon roasted
      garlic teriyaki sauce or soy sauce
2   teaspoons plus 1 teaspoon sherry
2   teaspoons cornstarch
1   pound flank steak, cut across the grain
      into thin 2- by 1-inch strips

1½ tablespoons oil
2   medium mangos, peeled, pitted, and
      sliced into ¼-inch slices, available
      fresh or frozen
8   warm flour tortillas

Mix the 1 tablespoon soy or teriyaki sauce, 2 teaspoons sherry, cornstarch, and steak in a glass bowl. Marinate 5 minutes. Heat the oil in a nonstick skillet or wok and stir-fry over high heat until meat is brown. Add remaining 1 tablespoon soy or teriyaki sauce and 1 teaspoon sherry. Stir 30 seconds. Add mango and heat through. Place some of meat mixture on each tortilla and wrap up like a burrito. Serve with salsa and black beans. Yield: 4 servings

GOLF TIP: Chipping with your 3 wood works best when your ball lies no more than a foot into the first cut of rough.

OUT OF BOUNDS BURRITOS

Great for a casual dinner or teenagers' party.

1   (3 pound) tri-tip roast or flank steak
1½ cups salsa
1   onion, chopped
1   bell pepper, chopped

½   cup beef broth
    Salt
12 corn or flour
        tortillas

Put all the ingredients except tortillas in a crockpot and cook 8 to 10 hours on low. Remove the meat, shred with a fork. Return the meat to the sauce and cook until warm. Taste for salt. Serve the meat in warm tortillas with cheese, chopped tomatoes, and blue cheese salad dressing. Yield: 6 servings

GOLF TITLES: In 1997 Annika Sorenstam led the LPGA in tournament victories and prize money but failed in her attempt to win a third consecutive U.S. Women's Open.

GRAND SLAM SAUSAGE
AND PEPPERS IN CRUSTY BREAD

1 loaf crusty Italian bread, sliced in half
    lengthwise
1 pound sweet Italian sausages
2 large bell peppers, cut into 1-inch strips

1 garlic clove, crushed
    Salt and pepper
2 teaspoons olive oil

Preheat oven to 350 degrees. Put bread in oven to warm for 10 minutes. In a nonstick skillet cook the sausages until done. Remove from the skillet and set aside. Pour off all but 2 teaspoons grease and cook the pepper strips and garlic until pepper is crisp-tender. Season with salt and pepper. Slice the sausages into 1-inch lengths and add to the peppers. Pull a little of the bread dough out of the center on both pieces to make room for the sausage. Brush the bread with 2 teaspoons olive oil. Pile the sausage and peppers onto one half and top with the other half. Cut crosswise into 4 pieces. Yield: 4 servings

GOLF CURIOSITY: Unusual caddies at Talamore at Pinehurst, North Carolina are llamas. They carry 2 bags and cost $100 per round (including handler).

PAR 5 CHEESEBURGER

You had the lowest score, so you invite the gang over for beer and burgers.
This one is easy. It bakes in the oven while you discuss the game.

1 pound extra lean ground beef	2 cups corn flakes, crushed
1 teaspoon salt	½ cup evaporated milk
¼ teaspoon pepper	2 10-inch loaves (1 pound) brown 'n
1 tablespoon Worcestershire sauce	serve French bread, cut in half
¼ cup catsup	horizontally
¼ cup chopped onions	2 cups shredded cheddar cheese

Preheat oven to 375 degrees. Combine all the ingredients except the bread and cheese.
On the cut side of each of the unbaked bread quarters spread ¼ of the meat mixture. Bake
for 25 minutes. Sprinkle with the cheese. Bake 5 minutes longer. Slice to serve. Yield: 8 to
10 servings

GOLF RULES: Tee-shots must be struck from within a rectangle 2 club lengths in depth, but
players may stand outside it to hit their shots.

THE OVERSIZE

Not a large club, but a man-size mouth-watering burger.

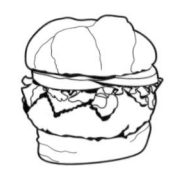

3   pounds ground sirloin
2   cups minced onion
2   cups diced bell pepper
2   cups peeled, seeded, and chopped
       tomatoes
½   cup chopped stuffed
       olives
3   cups shredded cheddar
       cheese
1½ teaspoons salt

Thoroughly mix all the ingredients and shape into 6 thick patties. Grill, broil, or pan-broil until desired doneness 10 to 12 minutes on each side for medium. Serve on toasted jumbo buns. Yield: 6 generous servings

GOLF POSTURE: In golf it is perfectly acceptable to stick your rear end out.

BOGEY-FREE BURGERS
WITH A WEDGE OF ROQUEFORT

Twenty minute gourmet burgers!

1 pound extra lean ground beef
¼ pound wedge Roquefort or blue
    cheese, crumbled
2 tablespoons prepared mustard

1 tablespoon soft butter
½ teaspoon garlic salt
¼ teaspoon pepper

Shape the meat into 4 patties ½-inch thick. In a nonstick skillet over high heat cook the patties until done (about 4 minutes for medium) turning once. While the meat is cooking mix the Roquefort cheese, mustard, butter, garlic salt, and pepper until smooth. Top each meat patty with ¼ of the cheese mixture. Cover with a lid and cook over low heat until the cheese is melted. Serve open-face on a slice of toasted French bread. Yield: 4 servings

GOLF HEALTH: Most sunglasses are not shatterproof when hit with a golf ball fired at high speed. Ask your optician to outfit your glasses and sunglasses with polycarbonate lenses. You should be able to find these safer lenses for about $30 more than you would pay for other types of plastic lenses.

ONE PUTT PIZZA

A 30 minute pizza with the great flavor of Philly cheese steak sandwiches.

1   pound extra lean ground beef
1   small bell pepper, cut into thin strips
1   small onion, thinly sliced and
    separated into rings
1   medium tomato, diced, and juice
    drained

¾   teaspoon salt
¼   teaspoon pepper
1   (12-inch) Italian bread shell
2   cups shredded mozzarella cheese

Preheat oven to 400 degrees. In a large nonstick skillet over medium heat brown the ground beef. Add the bell pepper and onion and cook 3 minutes. Add the tomato and cook 1 minute more. Season with salt and pepper. Place bread shell on baking sheet. With a slotted spoon arrange the beef and vegetables on top of the shell. Sprinkle with the cheese. Bake for 8 to 10 minutes or until cheese is melted. Yield: 8 slices

GOLF QUOTATION: "Ninety percent of putts that are short don't go in."

Yogi Berra

PEBBLE BEACH PINEAPPLE PIZZA

½ cup sweet and sour sauce
1 (12-inch) Italian bread shell
1 small bell pepper, cut into thin strips

2 ounces cooked ham, cut into thin strips
1 cup pineapple tidbits, well drained
1 cup shredded mozzarella cheese

Preheat oven to 450 degrees. Spread the sweet and sour sauce evenly over the bread shell. Arrange the bell pepper, ham, and pineapple over the sauce. Sprinkle with the cheese. Bake for 8 to 10 minutes. Serve immediately. Yield: 4 servings

GOLF QUOTATION: At the 1974 U.S. Open at Wingfoot Golf Club (called the massacre at Wingfoot) Hubert Green yelled to Lanny Watkins over in the rough, "It can't be too bad a lie. I can see your knees."

PAR 4 TURKEY, AVOCADO, AND CHEESE MELTS

The girls are coming over for lunch before your tee time.

6 English muffins, split	2 large tomatoes, sliced
Soft butter	12 slices Jack cheese
½ onion, diced fine, optional	12 slices deli roasted turkey breast
1 container frozen guacamole, thawed	

Preheat the broiler. Spread butter on the muffin halves. Toast under the broiler. Mix the onion and guacamole and spread on each muffin half. Add a slice of tomato and turkey, and top with a slice of cheese. Broil until the cheese melts. Add a bowl of soup to round out the menu. Yield: 12 melts

GOLF TRAVEL: The ultra exclusive Shadow Creek in Las Vegas is open to limited public play. One thousand dollars gets you a round of golf and a suite at the Mirage or Golden Nugget.

"PUT A SPIN ON THE BALL"
SHRIMP SALAD IN PITA POCKETS

½ pound cooked salad shrimp
½ cup chopped celery
2 tablespoons chopped onion
⅓ cup light mayonnaise
2 tablespoons capers, drained

¼ cup sliced olives
1 tablespoon lemon juice
  Salt and pepper
2 cups shredded lettuce
4 round pita bread, cut in half

Mix the shrimp, celery, onion, mayonnaise, capers, olives, lemon juice, salt, and pepper. Fold in the lettuce. Fill the halves of the pita bread with the shrimp salad. Yield: 4 to 8 servings

GOLF TRAVEL: There are over 95 golf courses near Myrtle Beach, S.C. There is nowhere that comes close to Myrtle Beach for such a great supply of high-quality golf.

QUICK CLUBHEAD ROLLS

Your father-in-law is coming to dinner—he loves rolls,
but don't let the rest of the family see them or he won't get any!

2   cups self-rising flour   Milk
¼   cup mayonnaise

Preheat oven to 400 degrees. Spray a 12-cup muffin tin with no-stick cooking spray. Mix the flour and mayonnaise and add ¾ to 1 cup milk until a soft sticky dough is formed. Spoon into muffin tins and bake for 15 minutes. Yield: 12 rolls

GOLF STUDS: In 1996 *Cosmopolitan Magazine* named Justin Leonard one of the 25 most eligible bachelors in the world.

DESERT INN DEVILED BISCUITS

A quick and easy snack biscuit to go with soups or salads.

1	package (10) refrigerated biscuits	1	can (4 ounces) deviled ham
¼	cup butter or margarine	¼	cup grated Parmesan cheese

Preheat oven to 425 degrees. Snip each biscuit into quarters with kitchen shears. Arrange in 2 (8-inch) round pans. Melt the butter and deviled ham in a small saucepan, stirring to blend, and pour over the biscuits, coating each one. Sprinkle with Parmesan cheese. Bake for 15 minutes. Serve hot. Yield: 40 biscuits

GOLF TRAVEL: Proof of handicap is required to play not only St. Andrews, but most of the top courses in the U.K. The handicap limit for the Old Course is 28 for men and 36 for women.

FAT SHOT CHEESE BREAD

1 small loaf (10-inch) French bread, sliced in half lengthwise	1 can (4 ounces) diced green chiles, drained
2 tablespoons olive oil	½ cup grated Parmesan cheese

Preheat oven to 350 degrees. Arrange the bread halves cut side up on a baking sheet. Combine the olive oil and chiles and spread over the bread halves. Sprinkle with the cheese. Bake for 20 minutes until hot and cheese is golden brown. Yield: 6 servings

GOLF GREATS: In 1996 Jack Nicklaus won his 100th tournament with a closing 65.

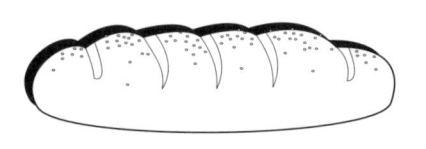

HOLE #9

The Sweet Spot (desserts)

STRATEGY ORANGE SUGAR RING COFFEE CAKE

Your partner is coming over to plan strategy for the club tournament.
You need coffee and something sweet.

2   packages (8 ounces each) refrigerator
        biscuits
¼   cup melted butter
2   tablespoons orange juice

½   cup sugar
½   cup brown sugar, firmly packed
1   teaspoon grated orange rind, optional
¼   teaspoon ground nutmeg

Preheat oven to 450 degrees. Combine the butter and orange juice. Mix together the sugars, orange rind and nutmeg. Dip the biscuits in the butter and then the sugar. Stand upright in a 1½-quart ring mold or bundt pan that has been sprayed with no-stick cooking spray. Bake for 15 minutes. Turn out on a plate. Yield: 1 ring

G◯LF CELEBRITY: John Denver, a singer who died in a plane crash in 1997, was a frequent participant in the AT&T Pebble Beach National Pro-Am.

BANANA BALL (SLICED) BANANAS

A Caribbean side dish to accompany spicy foods, such as Wailea Kalua Pork.

6	large firm bananas	⅓	cup brown sugar
1	cup orange juice	¼	teaspoon allspice
2	tablespoons lime juice		Butter

Preheat oven to 350 degrees. Peel the bananas, slice in half lengthwise, and place in a shallow baking dish. Add the orange and lime juice, sugar, and allspice. Dot with butter. Bake for 20 to 25 minutes until lightly browned. Yield: 6 to 12 servings

GOLF HERO: At the Asia Honda Classic 1997 in Thailand about 3,000 people chanted Tiger Wood's name as he sank a putt to win the $50,000 prize. Tiger has become a national hero in Thailand, birthplace of his mother.

ICE CREAM GREENHOPPERS

Impress your golfing buddies with this fancy dessert. Don't tell them how easy it is.

8 chocolate wafers	1 tablespoon green crème de menthe
1 pint slightly soft vanilla ice cream	

In a blender or food processor blend the wafers to fine crumbs. With a mixer at low speed beat the ice cream and crème de menthe until blended. In 4 fancy freezer-safe dessert glasses layer the ice cream mixture and chocolate crumbs. Freeze until ready to serve. Yield: 4 servings

G◯LF TRAVEL: Kiawah Island Resort's Ocean Course has been dubbed the "Toughest Resort Course in America".

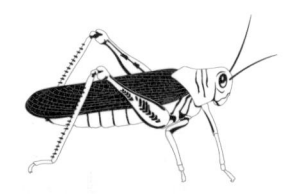

BOURBON GOLF BALLS

You can make these 2 weeks ahead.

1 cup plus ½ cup powdered sugar
1 box (12 ounces) vanilla wafers, finely
    crushed
1 cup finely chopped walnuts

6 tablespoons bourbon
2 tablespoons cocoa
3 tablespoons corn syrup

Mix 1 cup powdered sugar with the rest of the ingredients. Sprinkle ½ cup powdered sugar onto wax paper. Shape the dough into 1-inch balls and roll in the powdered sugar. Store in a tightly covered container. Yield: 3 dozen balls

GOLF HEALTH: To protect against skin cancer wear UV-protective sunglasses, don a broad-brimmed hat, and apply sunscreen on all exposed skin (including your lips) <u>before</u> you head for the course.

THE PINK SLICE

Preparation time—10 minutes, refrigeration time—overnight.

1 cup miniature marshmallows
1 package (10 ounces) frozen raspberries
   or strawberries
   Sugar

4 ounces low fat frozen
   whipped topping,
   thawed
1 angel food cake, sliced

Mix the marshmallows and the frozen berries in a bowl. Add sugar to taste if berries are not very sweet. Cover and refrigerate overnight. Before serving fold in the whipped topping. Serve on the angel food cake slices. Yield: 6 servings

GOLF EQUIPMENT: Harvey Penick believed that the most important clubs in the bag are the putter, the driver, and the wedge.

LADIES' TEE CHERRY TRIFLE

Preparation time 10 minutes. Refrigerate for 6 hours (time enough for 18 holes).

1   angel food cake, cut into 1-inch cubes
1   can (21 ounces) cherry pie filling
1   package (3.4 ounces) instant vanilla
     or lemon pudding

1½ cups milk
1   cup sour cream

Place ½ of the cake cubes in a 8 x 8 x 2-inch pan. Spread ⅔ of the pie filling over the cake. Cover with the rest of the cake. Combine the pudding mix with the milk and sour cream and beat until smooth. Pour over the cake. Refrigerate 6 hours. Garnish with the rest of the pie filling. Yield: 6 servings

GOLF GREATS: Arnold Palmer remains one of the most charismatic players. L.A. Times columnist, Jim Murray said of Palmer, "He swings like a man late for his daughter's wedding."

PEACH TOPPER BRUNCH TOAST

This is one time when it's O.K. to top it!

Crusty French bread, cut diagonally
   into 1-inch slices
Soft butter

Sugar
Peaches, peeled, cut into ¾-inch slices

Preheat oven to 425 degrees. Spread the bread slices with butter and sprinkle with sugar. Arrange 3 or 4 slices of peach on each slice of bread. Sprinkle with more sugar. Place on a cookie sheet. Bake on upper middle rack for 20 to 25 minutes until peaches are soft and bread is toasty. Serve while still warm. Yield: 1 or a crowd

G◯LF HISTORY: Bing Crosby, who once got down to a handicap of 2, died in 1977 after playing a round in Spain in the company of Manuel Pinero.

SWEET SPOT KAHLÚA SUNDAE

The girls from your league are coming for coffee. You forgot to buy a dessert.
No problem! You probably have these ingredients in the pantry.

4   tablespoons Kahlúa
4   scoops vanilla ice cream.
    Cocoa powder

Roasted pecans (roast
    10 minutes in a 350
    degree oven)

Place 1 scoop of ice cream in each of 4 pretty glasses. Pour 1 tablespoon Kahlúa over each scoop of ice cream, dust with cocoa, and garnish with pecans. Yield: 4 servings

GOLF GREATS: Patty Berg, together with Babe Zaharias and Betty Jameson, was one of the founders of the U.S. Women's Tour in which she became a dominant force.

CHOCOLATE DIVOTS

2   cups (12 ounces) milk chocolate chips   ½ cup raisins
1   tablespoon vegetable shortening   ½ cup chopped almonds

In a 1½-quart glass casserole microwave (high) the chocolate chips and vegetable shortening for 1½ to 2 minutes. Stir until smooth. Stir in the raisins and almonds. Drop by tablespoonfuls onto a wax paper-lined cookie sheet. Chill in the refrigerator until ready to serve. Yield: 2 dozen

GOLF RULES QUIZ: Should divots be replaced on the tees?

ANSWER: No, because a tee peg might shift in a loose divot.

GREAT PUTT PEANUT BUTTER PIE

1   cup crunchy peanut butter
1   cup sugar
1   package (8 ounces) reduced-fat
      cream cheese
1   teaspoon vanilla
2   teaspoons melted butter

1   tub (8 ounces) low fat frozen whipped
      topping, thawed
1   ready-to-use chocolate crumb pie crust
      (9-inch)
    Shaved chocolate or
      peanuts, optional

Beat the peanut butter, sugar, cream cheese, vanilla, and butter thoroughly until creamy. Fold in the whipped topping. Pour into the pie crust and refrigerate overnight or freeze for several hours. Garnish with shaved chocolate or peanuts. Yield: 1 (9-inch) pie

GOLF PASSION: In Dummerston, Vermont, in the winter of 1893, Rudyard Kipling took time out from writing by painting golf balls red and playing golf in the snow.

The SWEET SPOT

HOLE-IN-ONE DOUGHNUT SANDWICHES

Your grandchildren are coming over to celebrate your hole-in-one.
They will love this 10 minute dessert.

4   cake doughnuts, sliced in half
      lengthwise

1   milk chocolate candy bar
4   large marshmallows, cut in half

Put the doughnut halves on a microwave-safe plate. Lay pieces of the candy bar on 4 of
the halves. Lay 2 marshmallow halves on the other 4 doughnut halves. Heat in the microwave until the candy and marshmallows begin to melt about 15 to 20 seconds. Make
sandwiches by putting together a chocolate half and a marshmallow half. Yield: 4 servings

GOLF ETIQUETTE: The first player to hole out should be the one to replace the flagstick
after everyone has putted.

CHERRY HILLS CHOCOLATE CAKE

This cake goes together quickly.
The shiny chocolate frosting is delicious and takes just minutes to make.

2   eggs
1   package chocolate cake mix
1   can (21 ounces) cherry pie filling
5   tablespoons butter or margarine

⅓   cup milk
6   ounces semi-sweet chocolate chips
1   cup sugar

Preheat oven to 350 degrees. Beat the eggs, add the cake mix and pie filling, and beat until mixed. Pour into a bundt pan or 13 x 9-inch pan that has been sprayed with no-stick cooking spray. Bake for 50 minutes or until a toothpick inserted in the middle comes out clean. Cool. In the microwave melt the butter or margarine, milk, chocolate, and sugar in a microwave-safe bowl on high for 2 minutes, stirring every 30 seconds. Pour over the cake. Yield: 10 servings

GOLF RULES: Can a player share a club with his partner?

ANSWER: Yes. Rule 4-4b provides that partners may share clubs, but they may only do so if the total number carried by the partners is not more than 14.

DON'T CHOKE (IT'S ONLY A GAME) CHOCOLATE PIE

Put this pie together in the morning and let it freeze while you have a hot round.

4 ounces Sweet German chocolate	1 tub (8 ounces) low fat frozen whipped topping, thawed
⅓ cup milk	1 ready-to-use (9-inch) chocolate or graham cracker crumb pie crust
2 tablespoons sugar	
1 package (3 ounces) cream cheese, at room temperature	

Heat the chocolate with 2 tablespoons of the milk over low heat. Stir until melted. Beat the sugar into the cream cheese. Add remaining milk and chocolate mixture. Beat until smooth. Fold in the whipped topping. Pour into crumb pie crust. Freeze at least 4 hours. Garnish with chocolate candy sprinkles. Yield: 1 (9-inch) pie

GOLF WINNERS: Nearly half of the winners of PGA tournaments in 1997 were at least 6-feet 2-inches tall.

GOLF BAG PEANUT BUTTER CRUNCH

A great energy snack to take along in your golf bag.

2½ cups sugar
1½ cups white corn syrup

3 cups peanut butter, warmed in the microwave
12 cups corn flakes

Spray a 15½ x 10½-inch pan with no-stick cooking spray. Combine sugar and syrup in a saucepan. Bring to a fast boil stirring constantly. Do not over-cook. Remove from heat and add peanut butter. Stir until well mixed. Pour over corn flakes in a large bowl, and working quickly, mix well. Pour into prepared pan, pressing firmly. Cut into squares. Yield: 2 dozen bars

GOLF QUOTATION: "C'mon Bing (Crosby), wherever you are. Stop the rain." Tom Watson when rain was threatening suspension of play in the 1997 AT&T National Pro-Am tournament that Bing Crosby had brought to the Monterey Peninsula in California in 1947.

"TAP IN" CHOCOLATE CHIP CANDY

*You're suppose to bring a dessert to the church bake sale tonight,
but you're out of flour and tee time is in one hour.*

2   sticks butter
1   cup sugar
    Saltine crackers

1   bag (10 ounces) peanut butter or
      butterscotch chips
1   bag (12 ounces) chocolate chips

Preheat oven to 450 degrees. Line a cookie sheet with aluminum foil and place a single layer of saltines on it. In a medium saucepan melt the butter and the sugar stirring constantly. Pour the butter/sugar mixture over the crackers and bake for 7 minutes. Sprinkle with the peanut butter and chocolate chips. Put back into turned off oven long enough to partially melt the chips. Freeze until hard and break up into small pieces. Yield: 2½ pounds

G⊙LF FEES: As a rule of thumb, the more expensive the green fees, the more difficult the course.

NEED A GIFT FOR A GOLFER ??

BIRTHDAY

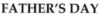

FATHER'S DAY

CHRISTMAS

MOTHER'S DAY

Turn the page for an order form

(Order now while supplies last)

To Order Copies of **THE GOLF COOKBOOK:**

Please send: _____ copies of *The Golf Cookbook* @ 10.95 each to:

Name: _____

Address: _____

City: _____ State: _____ Zip Code: _____

Telephone: (_____) _____

Sales Tax: Please add 85¢ per book for books shipped to California addresses.

Shipping: Enclose $2.00 for the first book and $1 for each additional book.

Make checks payable to *Redbank Ranch* and send orders to:

Redbank Ranch
10683 E. Bullard Ave
Clovis, CA 93611
(559) 323-9888